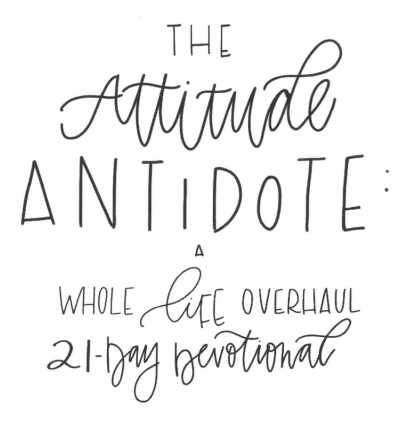

THE Attitude ANTIDOTE:

A WHOLE Life OVERHAUL 21-Day Devotional

Jessa Nowak

Cover illustration and chapter opening illustrations Copyright © 2018 by Allie Lloyd of Southern Scribe
Author Photo © Kristin Perry, back cover
Editor: Bonnie Lyn Smith

ISBN: Print: 978-0-692-15954-5 | eBook: 978-0-692-16112-8

Scripture quotations are taken from the Holy Bible, New Living Translation, copyright ©1996, 2004, 2015 by Tyndale House Foundation. Used by permission of Tyndale House Publishers, Inc., Carol Stream, Illinois 60188. All rights reserved.

I dedicate this book to my husband, two daughters, and my
Savior, Jesus Christ.

It is because of them I have begun this journey to better my
own attitude and change once and for all.

I am forever thankful for their patience with my growth. Their
love will always pull me through.

Table of Contents

INTRODUCTION   vii

DAY 1: CHANGE YOUR ATTITUDE, CHANGE YOUR LIFE   1

DAY 2: ATTITUDE IS A CHOICE   7

DAY 3: YOUR CHARACTER   13

DAY 4: EMOTIONAL CONTAGION   19

DAY 5: FINDING OPPORTUNITY IN THE CHALLENGE   25

DAY 6: FINDING PEACE   29

DAY 7: FINDING HAPPINESS IN CHRIST   35

DAY 8: APPRECIATE LIFE   41

DAY 9: PURPOSE FOR THE FIGHT   47

DAY 10: YOUR POWERFUL ROLE   51

DAY 11: THE SPIRIT'S GIFTS   57

DAY 12: MANIFESTED EMOTIONS   63

DAY 13: SELF-CONTROL   69

DAY 14: ATTITUDE OF CHRIST   75

DAY 15: REACTING WITH GRACE AND MERCY   81

DAY 16: ANGER   87

DAY 17: PRIDE   93

DAY 18: YOUR PAST   99

DAY 19: FEAR AND WORRY   105

DAY 20: PLANNED PRAYER   111

DAY 21: YOUR FUTURE   117

Introduction

"The key to friendship with God is not changing what you do, but changing your attitude toward what you do." —Brother Lawrence

*I*f you're reading this book, I'm certain there is a part of you that feels lost. Everyone feels lost at one point or another. Don't forget this: You are not alone in your struggles. Hope comes when you stop fooling yourself into thinking that the struggles are completely negative. Any situation that prompts self-improvement and growth is nothing to be ashamed of. It's actually something to be grateful for!

With the help of the Holy Spirit and this devotional guide, you will accomplish much. At the end of this 21-day journey, my hope for you is to increase your self-control, to discover joy and hope, to deal with past hurts and resentments, to refocus your life on what really matters, and ultimately to change your attitude and yourself from the inside out.

Be joyful! You are choosing to search for an answer through the power of Jesus Christ. You've found the ultimate solution because His path is truly the only way to have a fighting chance in accomplishing lasting change. For Christ, your healer, is searching for you and is ready and willing to make all things new (Revelation 21:5).

I have prayed for you throughout the composition of this book. And I promise to continually pray for you each day of your 21-day journey as you seek the peace only Jesus can offer.

"May God give you more and more grace and peace as you grow in your knowledge of God and Jesus our LORD." (2 Peter 1:2) I have the utmost confidence in you and your intentions to transform your character. Enjoy this journey!

All verses quoted here are from the New Living Translation version of the Bible.

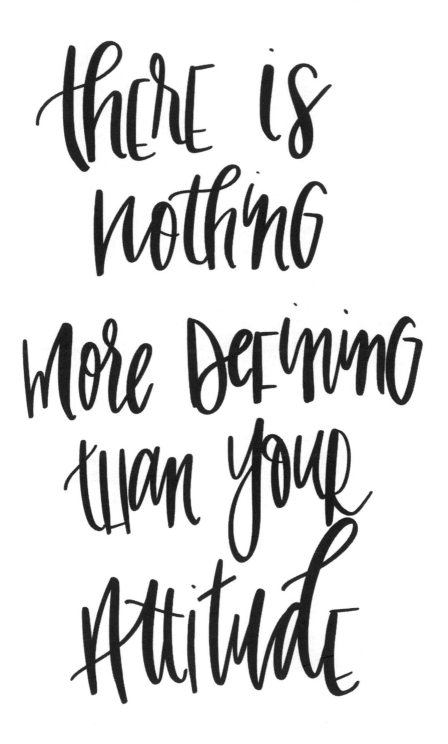

there is nothing More Defining than your Attitude

Day 1:
Change Your Attitude,
Change Your Life

There is nothing more defining than your attitude.

Why is it so difficult to consistently keep a good attitude? Because we don't always feel good on the inside. And what is felt on the inside will blossom outside, sooner or later. If attitudes were physically visible on your skin, would you be beautiful by society's standards? It's a hard question to answer. Often, bad attitudes steal our happiness and zest for life. This is no way to live! Please beware: Masking an attitude with a beautiful face is just as harmful as it is without the facade.

You will be consumed with resentment if you continue to hide true feelings and to portray an "everything's fine" appearance. "Kill them with kindness" is a phrase I'm sure you've heard. We usually use this motto when anger is raging inside but our attitude is completely the opposite (through clenched teeth). What ends up happening, though, is that we end up harming ourselves because we're living a lie. So does this mean to outwardly display everything we feel? No. The answer lies in changing how we feel on the inside to truly change our attitudes. The only way to do this is with the help of our Creator.

The collective self is made up of two inter-working parts: your inner self and outer self. Your inner self is how you feel—your emotions, peacefulness-to-anxiety ratio, reactivity rate, and overall well-being. Your outer self is essentially your inner self on display. Manifested feelings, including reactions, nonverbal gestures, facial expressions, and tone of voice, all culminate to form your attitude as a whole.

This book is about finding a way to manage and ultimately change your inner self, to effectively alter your thoughts and feelings about life. Subsequently, your outer self will then accurately reflect this beneficial change. You can then merge gentle truth and kindness into your relationships without fighting back a toxic attitude. No longer will you be a person who feels one way and acts another. My prayer for you is that your soul and your actions will be one with each other and that you will find peace.

Speaking of, have you ever really felt peace? It's a funny question, but once you consistently experience true peace, it will change you. Think back to a time when you sat down and looked at the world around you and simply smiled. When there were no thoughts or worries racing in your head despite the outside circumstances. When you were present in the moment and were content and happy with life. Some have never felt this kind of peace, while others have lost its powerful touch.

I encourage you to make this the goal for your day-to-day life. It is attainable—with the Prince of Peace. The first hurdle is knowing what it is you are looking for and spending daily time with Him. This is the attitude antidote. Congratulations! Today is the first day on your journey to find peace!

I truly believe your attitude and relationships will be changed for the better if you maneuver through this book with the help of Christ and the Holy Spirit. I encourage you to commit to meeting with the LORD through this book daily. Be warned: You will face challenges and situations that will try to push you away from this goal. Open your eyes to see the opposition that evil is throwing your way. Hold steadfast.

After all, "…if God is for us, who can ever be against us?" (Romans 8:31)

There is nothing more defining than your attitude.

LORD,

My attitude defines who I am. So God, it only hurts me when I label myself with anger and negativity. Let me shine Your light instead! I believe I can change. I know You are here to carry me through this journey. Creator, I ask that You reshape my heart, mind, and soul with Your perfect love.

Father, You created me. You know my inmost being. Why is it that I am faced with this struggle of keeping a good attitude? Whatever the reason, I pray that You will share Your wisdom with me. I pray that facing my challenge makes me a better person.

Jesus, I know the only way to attain peace in this world is through You. I want and need Your peace in my life. Please forgive all the rotten evilness inside me and replace it with love, compassion, patience, and kindness. Let peace flow like a mighty river through my veins. Only You, holy Prince of Peace, can give me this gift.

You are for me, so who could be against me? How encouraging, my Creator! God, You are for me because You have given me Jesus. God, You are for me because You have forgiven me. God, You are for me because You have gifted me with Your Spirit. I am forever grateful. I am forever in Your debt. Holy Spirit, with Your divine presence, I believe You have power to change me from the inside. LORD, I ask for Your help to keep me encouraged throughout this journey I am taking to better myself and those around me.

I pray for steadfastness as I embark on this challenge of eliminating a bad attitude from my life. God, help me be happy, joyful, loving, patient, and kind. Let the outside forces that try to stop me from reaching these goals be met by Your holy sword and shield. LORD, I know that with You this is possible.

God, thank you for listening to me. Thank you for forgiving and always loving me. Thank you for Your constant presence and for the power of Your grace to assist me in being more of who I was made to be. I ask You to be at the center of my life as I move throughout this day. As always, let Your angels watch over my family and me, keeping us safe. Let Your kingdom come; let Your will be done.

Amen,

Your Humbled Child

CHANGE *your* ATTITUDE CHANGE *your* LIFE

Day 2:
Attitude Is a Choice

*M*att loves sports, and he loves the Cubs even more. His dedication runs so deep that he hasn't missed seeing a game since he was 12 years old. Nothing makes him happier than watching his team slaughter their opponent. Unfortunately, when the Cubs lose, Matt transforms into a grump. This would make sense; after all, he feels as if he is part of the team. But in reality, Matt's family are the real losers here. They are the ones who deal with the inevitable gloom-and-doom attitude that spills into the house when the Cubs don't attain victory.

Let's break this down. Matt makes a choice each time he gets into the game. He chooses to let an outside circumstance determine his mood and attitude (for good or for bad). This may seem outrageous and silly to some, but it's real for Matt. And surprisingly, most of us face the same challenge, only in a different way. Matt would argue that his mood most certainly is not his choice. But it is. *Any* attitude is a choice. You possess the capability to be fully in control of your attitude.

Thoughts create feelings. Feelings do not create thoughts. So if you can control your thoughts, you can directly control your feelings. This is the attitude antidote. If you're tired of feeling sad, worried, mad, or whatever it may be, change your thoughts right now.

Your thoughts can define your reality and generate your feelings. So instead of thinking with negative intention, worry, and anger, think positive, affirming thoughts. For example, begin today by saying, "I am happy, full of joy, and glad to be alive. I am thankful for my life, physical body, and family. I will have no worry today. I have an excellent attitude, and I am full of patience. God is with me, and He loves me." Statements like these will become your reality if you dedicate yourself to thinking this way. God has given you a powerful mind to create the life that you want.

"But you are not controlled by your sinful nature. You are controlled by the Spirit if you have the Spirit of God living in you. (And remember that those who do not have the Spirit of Christ living in them do not belong to him at all.) And Christ lives within you, so even though your body will die because of sin, the Spirit gives you life because you have been made right with God." (Romans 8:9-10)

The verse above reminds us that the Spirit can help us to achieve our thought-changing goals. We can be freed from our negative thoughts and controlled by the Spirit if we so choose. As an exercise today, write down 10 positive and affirming statements to read aloud. Keep this list with you. Read it often, as often as you need to keep negative thoughts away. Get yourself into the habit of doing this, and you not only will change your attitude, but you also will change your life.

Change your attitude, change your life.

I am loved, I am thankful for my family. I am happy and glad to be alive.

Jesus,

I have been made right with You due to Your selfless acts of love. Father, forgive me when I don't allow the Spirit to control my life and when I have let my sinful nature and negativity rule me instead. I no longer want to be a slave to my thoughts, which are so damaging to me and to those around me. My thoughts have created feelings of anxiety, worry, sadness, and distrust. I don't want to feel those emotions anymore! I long to be joyful, content, peaceful, appreciative and patient.

My attitude depends on the thoughts I permit to enter my mind, so Spirit, I need You and humbly ask You to rule over my thoughts. Every moment of the day, I need Your divine intervention in stopping my typical thought pattern. My help comes from You, the one who made heaven and earth. How awesome is Your name! I need Your grace today, yesterday, and tomorrow.

Creator, You have gifted me such a beautiful life full of love and opportunity. I often take the time You have provided me and use it negatively. Forgive me for choosing to have an awful attitude when I let outside circumstances affect me. I have chosen to infect others with my ugliness and have been an active destroyer of good whenever I allow myself to have a negative attitude. Forgive me, Father, for choosing this! I promise to start using the life You've given me for good.

Spirit, I need You in my hardest times. I beg for Your help so I may not let outside circumstances change me. Help me to be steadfast and strong in the face of struggle. God, reveal to me whatever it is that I need to help me make better decisions.

Today as I use affirmations to change my thought patterns, I pray that You will motivate my efforts. Let no evil thing come between me and the good thoughts that will change my life for the better. I know the devil and his army will be out to sabotage my efforts, but I will have no fear, for I know that You are near. I know

You will stand by my side and fight for me. Thank you for loving me, LORD.

God, thank you for listening to me. Thank you for forgiving and always loving me. Thank you for Your constant presence and for the power of Your grace to assist me in being more of who I was made to be. I ask You to be at the center of my life as I move throughout this day. As always, let Your angels watch over my family and me, keeping us safe. Let Your kingdom come; let Your will be done.

Amen,

Your Humbled Child

It's impossible to have a bad attitude with good character

Day 3:
Your Character

The most valuable part of ourselves is our character. Merriam-Webster defines it as "one of the attributes or features that make up and distinguish an individual." Our thoughts, feelings, attitude, words, reactions, and actions define who we are as people and constitute our character. Today, there is little talk about fostering character development at all. It seems the world tends to overlook the notion of goodness as a whole. But not us! We will be the change in the world, for we are difference makers!

A wise person once taught me that each little decision made on a daily basis results in a larger defining action. All in all, over time, small changes add up to monumental change. Take Tracy's story, for example. Tracy would occasionally smoke a cigarette in social settings, but after her divorce, she began to smoke one cigarette at the end of her day to calm her emotions. Having the cigarettes around were an obvious temptation, so she would often choose to smoke one in the morning and one at night. She would never have considered herself a real "smoker," but if you add up the cigarettes, she smoked nearly a whole pack in two weeks. All of a sudden, based on her small, seemingly infrequent decisions, she would be coined a smoker. You may not smoke, but be careful not to judge her, for this situation can be applied in various contexts to anyone.

Bottom line: For better or for worse, we become the culmination of each small decision we make. Sometimes, unknowingly, we may end up a smoker, or someone who is rude, always late, or negative. Thankfully, this principle applies not only to bad traits but also to good ones. When dutifully focused, our actions help us become people who are generous, thoughtful, sweet, helpful, and nice to be around. First Peter and the book of Colossians give us some positive character attributes to focus on in order to have the character that God has called us to. Just as Tracy's small daily decisions began to define her, our good decisions add up to shape us into better people with outstanding character.

"Finally, all of you should be of one mind. Sympathize with each other. Love each other as brothers and sisters. Be tenderhearted, and keep a humble attitude. Don't repay evil for evil. Don't retaliate with insults when people insult you. Instead, pay them back with a blessing. That is what God has called you to do, and he will grant you his blessing." (1 Peter 3:8-9)

If our focus shifts to character development, there will be no room for a negative attitude of any kind. Instead of concentrating on avoiding an attitude today, we can focus on improving our character to achieve the same result in a more positive way. Our attitude will naturally follow suit. This is the attitude antidote.

"Since God chose you to be the holy people he loves, you must clothe yourselves with tenderhearted mercy, kindness, humility, gentleness, and patience. Make allowance for each other's faults, and forgive anyone who offends you. Remember, the LORD forgave you, so you must forgive others. Above all, clothe yourselves with love, which binds us all together in perfect harmony. And let the peace that comes from Christ rule in your hearts. For as members of one body you are called to live in peace. And always be thankful." (Colossians 3:12-15)

To transform your character, take to heart these five principles and begin to incorporate them into your life as soon as possible. For it's impossible to have a bad attitude when focusing on good character.

1. **React like Jesus.** Remember the famous W.W.J.D. (*What Would Jesus Do?*) bracelets? Before reacting to someone or something, keep in mind how Jesus would react. Most likely, He would have an even-tempered, loving, and perhaps wise and witty response to even the harshest comment. In fact, He would exhibit perfect mercy, kindness, humility, gentleness, and patience.

2. **Be sincerely interested in others.** We are called to connect with others and to spread God's love. If you tend to keep to yourself, try opening up and talking to someone you don't know today. Make it a goal to touch or affect someone else's life each day for the better.

3. **Be willing to help others.** If someone needs something, be the person to do it. Offer your support in any way that you can. Your time, money, or emotional support are all good deeds that will never be overlooked in God's eyes. Helping others will transform you.

4. **Forgive without a grudge.** No matter the offense, God expects and requires us to forgive willingly and graciously. No questions asked. In fact, He even says He won't forgive you if you don't fulfill this obligation (Matthew 6:15).

5. **Set yourself aside for others.** Humility is one of the defining features of Christ that should be valued and emulated. Being humble actually makes it easier to exhibit higher self-control in many situations. When in doubt, stop thinking about yourself and start thinking of the other person. It will drastically change your perspective and attitude. Better yet, your character and attitude will be in tip-top shape.

It's impossible to have a bad attitude with good character.

15

Christ in heaven,

You have lived the perfect life, died a horrific criminal's death that You did not deserve, and endured the depths of hell, all for the sake of Your children—all to forgive me for the poor decisions that I make on a daily basis. I realize that these decisions make up my character and define who I am.

LORD, I often dislike who I've become, as it is miles away from the character You displayed and how the Bible teaches me to live. I have hurt others, including You, with my thoughts, attitude, words, actions, and reactions. Please forgive my selfish nature and the hurt I have caused You and others through my character flaws, for I have not taken You and Your instruction into my daily decisions. Please forgive me and make me clean.

I ask that Your Holy Spirit comes into my life and motivates, reminds, and encourages me each minute of the day to have better character. I pray that my attitude will transform me through this process, as I believe it will. Create in me a new heart, LORD, and make my character the most beautiful thing about me. Let others be inspired by my Christ-like attitude, manner, and deeds. I wish to be a change-maker in the world.

Father, I ask that You inspire those around me to work on their character as well. For it is much easier to live in harmony with like-minded individuals. I pray that You bring people into my life who inspire me to make better decisions and who push me to become the person I was made to be. I know I will face opposition as I begin to focus on good character. Forces will try to bring me down, but I pray that Your angels will be here to help me up and keep me on the right path. Jesus, Your life inspires me to shine Your light. Spirit, please break down the walls and open the hearts of the people I decide to open up to. Let the Creator's light pierce their souls. Let me have an undeniable impact on their lives. Father in Heaven, Your will be done.

God, thank you for listening to me. Thank you for forgiving and always loving me. Thank you for Your constant presence and for the power of Your grace to assist me in being more of who I was made to be. I ask You to be at the center of my life as I move throughout this day. As always, let Your angels watch over my family and me, keeping us safe. Let Your kingdom come; let Your will be done.

Amen,

Your Humbled Child

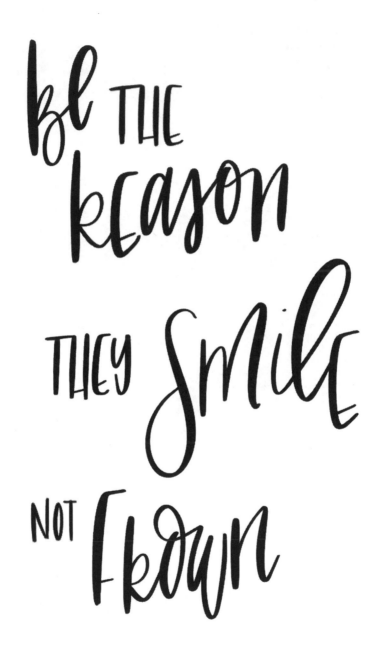

Day 4:
Emotional Contagion

*H*ow much time do you give to your mind to allow rest? If you're like the rest of us, it's not enough. I believe that one of the most prevalent harms today is the lack of respite time we allow our minds, bodies, and souls. A nonstop mentality and lifestyle affects our physical and mental health, our relationships, and our quality of life. Too much bustle without sufficient downtime negatively impacts every part of us, including our spirits and souls. Possibly most important of all, mental exhaustion puts stress on our closest relationships, including the one we have with Christ. When there is too much noise in our heads, it is exceedingly difficult, if not impossible, to hear the Holy Spirit. If schedules are packed full, where nearly every moment is filled, there is no time to take sufficient care of ourselves or our relationships.

We are all vitally connected in life, especially to those we spend the most time with. Imagine that your business partner or significant other arrives in a bad mood. Instantly, you feel your own mood changing. This is a normal phenomenon. It's more than empathy; it's called emotional contagion. We take on the emotions of others around us. This is wake-up call number one!

You have a direct effect on those around you. You play a very powerful role in your relationships. Even without saying one word, body language tells all. There is no hiding a bad mood from anyone—for long. Since it can't be hidden, it must change. If not, the negativity will ultimately affect others for the worse. Talk about motivation!

Jesus said, "Do to others whatever you would like them to do to you. This is the essence of all that is taught in the law and the prophets." (Matthew 7:12) We can find even further motivation in the Golden Rule, which came directly from Jesus. In essence, be the person you would want to be with. If you want your family and friends to be patient and to give you compassion, joyfully do those very things for them first. This is love. And love is transforming.

Connection is a natural human need; we want people to like us. We feed off the satisfaction that someone enjoys our company, wants to spend time with us, and loves us. So here's where it all comes together: No one, no matter how much they love you, wants to be around you when you're in what I like to call a "poody mood."

Make it a goal today to be the person your spouse fell in love with, the parent you wanted to have, the friend or coworker you long for, or the child God desires you to be. Focus your energy today on being someone others will want to spend time with. You can do it—you have it in you to be this person! This is the antidote to attitude. Decide to clear your mind, however you can, to do this. Utilize yoga or exercise, meditation, prayer, or enveloping yourself in loud music, reading, shopping, crying, or praying—whatever works for you. The people in your life are counting on you to keep the relationship strong and healthy for their own moods' sake!

"Don't be afraid, for I am with you. Don't be discouraged, for I am your God. I will strengthen you and help you. I will hold you up with my victorious right hand." (Isaiah 41:10)

God has promised us that He is with us. Give your worries and cares to Him. Ask Him to clear your mind, de-stress you, and revitalize you. He will help strengthen you.

God will be your most effective helper, so don't fret. After all, with God on your side, you've got all the power in the world.

Be the reason they smile, not frown.

Father!

Your beautiful promise gives me all the hope in the world. You have promised that You will be here in my struggle and will lift me up. I have been instructed not to be discouraged, as You and Your guiding Holy Spirit will lead me.

Heavenly Father, thank you for another beautiful day. I will choose to be a ray of energy today for You. I will be a shining light, energizing those around me. God, I believe I have the energy, motivation, and willpower to be this person. My family and friends will smile because of my presence, with Your help. Spirit, I ask You to fill my soul with Your inspiring joy.

My creator, You have made me in Your likeness to connect with others. Please forgive me for often adding negativity to others' lives instead of being the hope and happiness they crave. My relationships mean so much to me, and I want to be the reason they smile, not frown. Jesus, You have instructed me to do to others what I would like them to do to me. I will choose to follow Your Word.

LORD, You have purposed me with great gifts. Let those gifts shine into others' lives. Let me enjoy those gifts, God. My stress, LORD, is often inhibitory. But You have instructed me to cast all my cares on You. Declutter my brain, de-stress my body, refresh my soul, and allow me to enjoy the beautiful world you've created around me. Open my eyes to the beauty. I cast all my cares on You! LORD, I am counting on You to lighten my load and lift me up today.

God, thank you for listening to me. Thank you for forgiving and always loving me. Thank you for Your constant presence and for the power of Your grace to assist me in being more of who I was made to be. I ask You to be at the center of my life as I move throughout this day. As always, let Your angels watch over my family and me, keeping us safe. Let Your kingdom come; let Your will be done.

Amen,

Your Humbled Child

THE bigger YOUR CHALLENGE the MORE Opportunity FOR GROWTH

Day 5:
Finding Opportunity in the Challenge

"Dear brothers and sisters, when troubles of any kind come your way, consider it an opportunity for great joy. For you know that when your faith is tested, your endurance has a chance to grow. So let it grow, for when your endurance is fully developed, you will be perfect and complete, needing nothing. If you need wisdom, ask our generous God, and he will give it to you. He will not rebuke you for asking. But when you ask him, be sure that your faith is in God alone. Do not waver, for a person with divided loyalty is as unsettled as a wave of the sea that is blown and tossed by the wind." (James 1:2-6)

What an incredible message of how to deal with adversity! We often wonder why things happen in life. After all, it seems as if there is always something going on that stirs the pot. While discussing the point of life's obstacles could be a book in itself, we see here that troubling times provide space for your personal growth. How incredible! If you are stressed out and are struggling to keep your patience and attitude under control on a daily basis, don't despair. This is your opportunity.

Many situations in life illustrate this point. Pruning is a necessary process that keeps a plant healthy and vibrant. The cutting away of dead or overgrown branches or stems, in turn, creates beautiful, more plentiful blossoms. Keep in mind that the initial pruning process makes the plant look exposed and bare—it requires an actual physical change. However, after a while, the plant bears new life and creates even more beauty than had once existed. Strength training as a workout requires the breakdown of current muscle. Old muscle tears and then repairs itself, resulting in a larger and stronger muscle. Precious metals are created through smelting, which involves continual melting to rid the metal of impurities. The repeating theme we see here is that in order to create something new, stronger, and more beautiful, the old must be removed. The removal process may be difficult at times, but the end result is worth it.

What's even more incredible is that James gives insight to the ultimate goal: fully developed endurance. It's attainable; what an inspiration! He is illustrating here your incredible potential! You have the God-given ability to reach a point in your personal growth journey where you are complete. I highly recommend that you read the full chapter of James 1 right now, as it provides much insight and content for inspired living. And speaking of endurance, James isn't the only one to speak of it.

"We can rejoice, too, when we run into problems and trials, for we know that they help us develop endurance. And endurance develops strength of character, and character strengthens our confident hope of salvation. And this hope will not lead to disappointment. For we know how dearly God loves us, because he has given us the Holy Spirit to fill our hearts with his love." (Romans 5:3-5)

Challenges, problems, issues—call them what you will—are actually good for you! Your character needs to be developed, and it simply can't be done without a fire. The bigger the challenge you face, the larger your growth potential is. This is the attitude antidote. Look at your fire with a different perspective. Change your glasses, and realize that you're not going anywhere in life without some sort of pressure. Appreciate it! And as crazy as it sounds, rejoice in the struggle. Remember, it's all in your perception.

The bigger the challenge, the more opportunity for growth.

Jesus,

Thank you for giving me such incredible insight to life's challenges. Your Word gives me hope that one day soon I will be able to grow out of this attitude problem that I face. Please forgive me for my poor attitude, when really, I have no reason to be acting like this. I need You to transform my heart, my head, and my soul. I believe You can change me. I have faith that one day I will no longer struggle with controlling my negativity. In my future, I see a person who is happy, patient, and kind on a daily basis.

Generous Creator, I need wisdom. I trust You will give it to me and not rebuke me for asking. My faith is in You alone. I now realize that when my faith is tested, my endurance has a chance to grow. So, please, protect my well-being and self-confidence when I am tested.

God, I need You. I need You when I'm mad. I need You when I'm hurting. I need You when I'm angered. The second I'm plagued with my attitude about to flare, I need You. Spirit, please step in and take over. Help me to stop losing control. I have full faith that You can and will honor my requests and change me from the inside.

Heavenly Father, You created me and my beautiful mind. I believe I can find opportunity in opposition and joy in the struggle. Carry me though this time of growth. Help my perception to be one of appreciation and opportunity for growth.

God, thank you for listening to me. Thank you for forgiving and always loving me. Thank you for Your constant presence and for the power of Your grace to assist me in being more of who I was made to be. I ask You to be at the center of my life as I move throughout this day. As always, let Your angels watch over my family and me, keeping us safe. Let Your kingdom come; let Your will be done.

Amen,

Your Humbled Child

PEACE:
trust in God
don't worry
PRAY ABOUT
everything
BE APPRECIATIVE
think
POSITIVE

Day 6:
Finding Peace

Something is missing in life, but you can't identify what it is. If you've ever experienced an empty feeling, as if there were a hole in your heart that just won't stay filled, you're not alone. That is God calling for you! That hollow sensation may manifest in feelings of sadness, uneasiness, loneliness, despair, anxiety, frustration, or depression—all which play a part in your attitude. But what is that feeling? It's the lack of peace and the lack of God's true company. If you've consistently felt any of the feelings described above, you're missing God's peace!

So how do we attain peace? Peace can only come from one place: Jesus Christ. Over and over the Bible speaks of the need to actively strive for peace. Recall that God promises that if we seek, we will find what we're looking for (Matthew 7:7-8). This is the attitude antidote.

"Always be full of joy in the LORD. I say it again—rejoice! Let everyone see that you are considerate in all you do. Remember, the LORD is coming soon. Don't worry about anything; instead, pray about everything. Tell God what you need, and thank him for all he has done. Then you will experience God's peace, which exceeds anything we can understand. His peace will guard your hearts and minds as you live in Christ Jesus. And now, dear brothers and sisters, one final thing. Fix your thoughts on what is true, and honorable, and right, and pure, and lovely, and admirable. Think about things that are excellent and worthy of praise. Keep putting into practice all you learned and received from me—everything you heard from me and saw me doing. Then the God of peace will be with you." (Philippians 4:4-9)

How absolutely incredible! Philippians gives us step-by-step instructions on how to attain God's peace. Let's break down all the instructions here:

1. **Trust in God.** He is the ultimate power, the Alpha and the Omega, ruler over heaven and earth. He has promised that if we love Him and work for His purpose, He will work all things for our good (Romans 8:28). And let's face it, if the ultimate authority is for us, then there is no reason not to give in and let Him rule.

2. **Don't worry.** Don't overthink this one. There is no changing how others act or what God's plans are no matter how much we worry. "And be sure of this: I am with you always, even to the end of the age." (Matthew 28:20b) Even during the difficult times, He is there. And truly, He is more concerned with our character development than our comfort.

3. **Pray about everything.** Prayer is our direct line to God. A healthy relationship requires constant communication. We must make it a happy habit and a priority to call and discuss life with the one who loves us most.

4. **Be appreciative.** We would have nothing without God's grace. Let us always remember how much we have and what an incredible future awaits us only because of the love of Jesus Christ.

5. **Think positively.** Our creator has gifted us with a very powerful tool—our minds. We can choose to walk the path of gratitude and positivity or the path of worry and fear. Our mindset matters in making our journey a happy one or one full of negative feelings.

It's fascinating how the Bible gives such good advice. Lately, positive thinking and changing mindsets have become the trendy topics to finding happiness. There are books, podcasts, blogs, and public speakers to teach you how to change your way of thinking. This is not new! The Holy Bible was the first to explain how to do just that. Simply, fix your thoughts on what is good and true. In other words, read the Bible, stop worrying, and focus on the good things in your life. Appreciate your family, friends, and all the blessings bestowed on you.

"I pray that God, the source of hope, will fill you completely with joy and peace because you trust in him. Then you will overflow with confident hope through the power of the Holy Spirit." (Romans 15:13)

Trust in God. Don't worry. Pray about everything. Be appreciative. Think positively.

Prince of Peace,

I hear You calling when I feel empty inside. For some reason, I often don't answer Your call, and for that, I fall on my knees and ask for forgiveness. I humbly realize that You are the only one who can fill this void inside my soul, so I pray You do just that. I desire an intimate, real relationship with You so I will be able to fully rely on You when trouble hits. I need Your Spirit to align my thoughts, feelings, actions, and life with You.

God, I struggle so much with my worries. I know that I need to be giving You my concerns, but it is so difficult sometimes when I feel as if my problems consume me. LORD, I don't want my circumstances to dictate my mood anymore. I know the only way to achieve peace is to seek You and to ask for the peace that only You can give. Please help me to get out of my own head and into Your realm of peace.

When I'm anxious about situations in life, please surround me with Your all-enveloping presence. Remind me that You are all I need and that You are in control. I need You to hold me and comfort me, LORD. Help me to keep my thoughts only on that which is true.

Creator, hear my heart down to the depths of my soul. I long to be always full of joy. Prince of Peace, please grant me Your gracious gift. I trust in You and choose to surrender my life to You. Forgive my selfish nature and my distrust. Day after day, I need Your peaceful presence in my life.

God, thank you for listening to me. Thank you for forgiving and always loving me. Thank you for Your constant presence and for the power of Your grace to assist me in being more of who I was made to be. I ask You to be at the center of my life as I move throughout this day. As always, let Your angels watch over my family and me, keeping us safe. Let Your kingdom come; let Your will be done.

Amen,

Your Humbled Child

GOD HAS A bigger + better plan THAN you HAVE for yourself

Day 7:
Finding Happiness in Christ

"So I concluded there is nothing better than to be happy and enjoy ourselves as long as we can. And people should eat and drink and enjoy the fruits of their labor, for these are gifts from God." (Ecclesiastes 3:12-13)

You cannot be happy with a negative attitude; it's as simple as that. Regardless of religion, age, or gender, everyone wants to find happiness. There are multitudes of philosophies and books written on this topic, and I'm not claiming to be a philosophical expert, but I will share with you my simple formula for becoming your happiest you.

The short of it? Connect with God every day. There is nothing of any value in this life without the goodness of our Creator. If there is, it is fleeting and will ultimately end with heartache. "Whatever is good and perfect is a gift coming down to us from God our Father, who created all the lights in the heavens. He never changes or casts a shifting shadow." (James 1:17)

Even if you love and accept Christ, we all have been guilty of living our lives without Him. It's so easy to become busy and move through your day without a thought, prayer, or mention. All of a sudden, overscheduled days snowball into crazy weeks, and you find yourself feeling a little empty. That empty feeling is the lack of God. He is calling for you! If left unanswered, that lack of something in your soul may manifest into feelings of depression, anxiety, worry, sadness, impatience, increased negativity, or simply feeling unsettled.

Make it a priority to meet with Jesus and connect with Him on a daily basis. It will make all the difference in your attitude, life, and level of happiness and contentment. This is the attitude antidote. Often, prayers can be a little unorganized, so always remember to include the most fundamental element of Christianity into your daily prayers. Whenever you meet with Him, confess your sins, ask for forgiveness, and believe it is done. Let Jesus's blood cleanse you each day and make your load lighter. "Oh, what joy for those whose disobedience is forgiven, whose sin is put out of sight!" (Psalm 32:1)

While meeting with Jesus in prayer, ask for happiness! If you do know what can make you happy, ask God specifically for that. If you don't know what will make you happy, pray for the answer until you figure it out. If you can't identify what it is that you want, your prayers cannot be answered! Once you've asked, you must then believe it will happen. Trust that God will answer your prayers! "And we are confident that he hears us whenever we ask for anything that pleases him. And since we know he hears us when we make our requests, we also know that he will give us what we ask for." (1 John 5:14-15) Lastly, be full of anticipation and gratitude for those answered prayers—even before they are.

Often, unhappiness can be associated with a lack of purpose. And just as happiness is reliant on being close to Jesus, finding purpose is too. "The LORD says, 'I will guide you along the best pathway for your life.   I will advise you and watch over you.'" (Psalm 32:8)

We all have plans for our lives, but if your plans benefit only the needs of you and your family, consider that your purpose may possibly be lacking God's vision. Remember, God loves you individually, yes, but He also has a whole world of people He cares for, and all things need to fit into His miraculous design. We are His ambassadors here, and it is our responsibility to help Him accomplish His plan. Just as you feel great joy in giving gifts, your happiness may emerge while assisting others in finding theirs. Jesus lived His whole life in servanthood; take heed, and consider trying to incorporate serving others into your purpose. (The chapter "The Spirit's Gifts" will further help you through this process.)

"For the Scriptures say, 'If you want to enjoy life and see many happy days, keep your tongue from speaking evil and your lips from telling lies. Turn away from evil and do good. Search for peace, and work to maintain it. The eyes of the LORD watch over those who do right, and his ears are open to their prayers. But the LORD turns his face against those who do evil.'" (1 Peter 3:10-12)

God has a bigger and better plan for your life than you have planned for yourself.

Jesus,

I ask that You turn Your face toward me. I don't deserve it, but I know You have given me this opportunity to meet with You because of Your incredible sacrifice. Take my ugliness away, and make me beautiful in Your sight once again. Jesus, I ask You to take my sin and erase it from my life. Let my temptations decrease each day as I grow firmer in my faith. I will do my best to do good and to turn away from evil. Please send your angels to assist me on a daily basis to help me accomplish this feat.

I will search for peace today and work to maintain it. LORD, I am so ashamed that I stumble so easily. I want to do so much better, and then I crumble under minimal pressure. Creator, I cry out to You: Refine me in Your fire! Make me resilient in Your image, for I am eager to be better. My attempts often fail miserably, but I know You are there to pick me up. Thank you for never giving up on me.

Father in heaven, Your love surrounds me, and because of that, I can find happiness here in this world. Help me be the spark that lights the fire in others' hearts. I pray that I see opportunity in the struggle and when others need You. Open my eyes to Your path for my life, as I know my narrow-minded vision pales in comparison to what You have in store for me. I want to fulfill my duty as a follower to help others find You. I know You are all that ultimately matters.

When I meet You face to face, LORD, I can only imagine I will fall to my knees. My heart yearns to be with You again in Your perfect all-encompassing love. When I meet You, I long to make You proud. It is my first and most important task to figure out how I can make that happen. Spirit, guide my soul toward the greater path that leads me where God intends me to be. Let all the surrounding noise dampen so I can hear Your voice. Let all the busyness blur in the background so I may see Your path light up in the chaos.

God while I am here, I wish to experience happiness every day, regardless of the circumstances. Take my burdens, and lighten my load, as only You, my Savior, can do. I ask for clarity on what exactly will make me happy. Assist me in seeing the bigger picture. I believe You will answer this and all my prayers, as I have full faith that You hear me. Thank you for loving me. Help me love others as You have demonstrated. Take my selfish nature and mold me into a person You will be proud of. I am a difference-maker, and I will stand for You, God.

God, thank you for listening to me. Thank you for forgiving and always loving me. Thank you for Your constant presence and for the power of Your grace to assist me in being more of who I was made to be. I ask You to be at the center of my life as I move throughout this day. As always, let Your angels watch over my family and me, keeping us safe. Let Your kingdom come; let Your will be done.

Amen,

Your Humbled Child

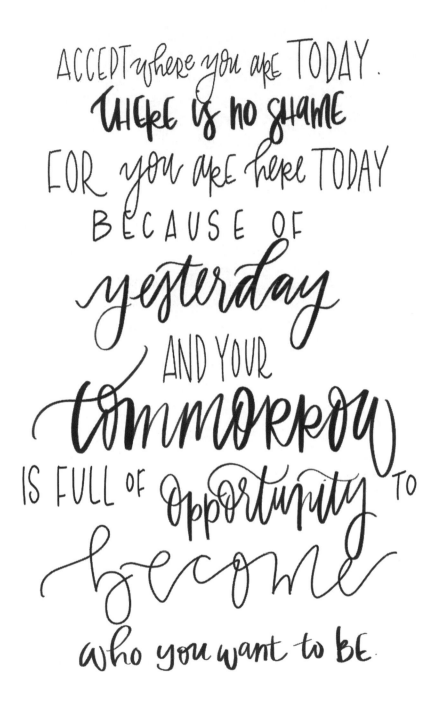

ACCEPT where you are TODAY.
THERE is no SHAME
FOR you are here TODAY
BECAUSE OF
yesterday
AND YOUR
tommorrow
IS FULL OF opportunity TO
become
who you want to BE.

Day 8:
Appreciate Life

*M*eet John. He was newly married to Sara and loved sports and life outdoors. He and Sara both worked full-time jobs that provided a nice living. At night they came home to their newly purchased home to be happily greeted by their new puppy. John's life was picture-perfect at the moment from the outside; however, something was amiss. The weekends would come, and he would begin to feel antsy. John quickly realized that he was mourning his old life, when weekends were all about football and friends and doing whatever he wanted to do. This new life seemed to bring a great deal of responsibility and stress to a once-carefree individual. Over time, he developed an attitude of contempt toward Sara. At the time he didn't know why he was unhappy, negative, and short on patience. Interactions with her would get under his skin, and he couldn't move past it.

John now explains that the early years of marriage were a huge challenge for him in accepting his new life. Day after day, he was determined to work through his feelings, asking God for help. Sara and he began to do devotions together. Then, one Sunday, while reading the story of Job, he broke down and cried. Job lost everything he had but was still faithful to God. John realized what it would be like if *he* lost everything, and suddenly all the pieces fell into place. He began to view his wife and their life together differently. Appreciation and acceptance of this new season of life filled his heart. He explains that he changed because his perception and daily thoughts changed.

When I hear John's version of the story, I see the Holy Spirit at work. The Spirit helps us adjust our lives, thoughts, and feelings when we need it the most—but only if we *want* to be changed. Whether you're experiencing feelings of despair, depression, anger, resentment, or anxiety, or you're edgy with everything going on in this life, don't give up. If you're able to change your perception and thoughts, your feelings will follow. Shift your thoughts with the help of the Spirit. This is the attitude antidote.

More often than not, we're moving through our day not recognizing any of the beauty all around us. Life moves so quickly with responsibilities, deadlines, chores, work, and irritations. (Obviously the list of daily life tasks could continue off the page.) But if our lives are hyper-focused on the tasks, we could miss the meaning of it all. In this state, it is much easier to become overwhelmed. Negative attitudes can spiral out of control.

Attempt to initiate balance and focus on the beauty and good in your life throughout moments of the day. Kids screaming? Thank God they have healthy lungs and bodies to be able to do that. Mentally step out of the situation, smile, and know they will soon be grown and one day you'll be longing for the chaos. Enjoy and savor their smallness now, for one day it will be gone. Stressed over work? Thank God you have a job and you're doing well for your family. If you feel the need to make a move in your career, feel blessed that you have the choice. And don't forget to remember your accomplishments— the ones from today, yesterday, and the ones you'll make in the future.

But what happens if you're not happy where you are in life, like John? Or worse: You're not happy with who you are? When you are having trouble loving yourself, it certainly clouds your appreciation and your ability to see beauty. The answer lies in acceptance, perception, and prayer. Remember, if you're able to change your perception and thoughts, your feelings will follow. "Always be joyful. Never stop praying. Be thankful in all circumstances, for this is God's will for you who belong to Christ Jesus." (1 Thessalonians 5:16-18)

Accept where you are today. This is who you are, and you are beautiful—struggles and all! There is no shame. For you are here today because of yesterday, and your tomorrow is full of opportunity to become whoever you choose. You can write your own future—how empowering! Accepting your current circumstances doesn't mean you will be there forever. Remember, there is beauty and opportunity in the struggle. No one is perfect, and you don't have to be either.

Accept where you are today. There is no shame. For you are here today because of yesterday, and your tomorrow is full of opportunity to become whomever you choose.

Giver of all things,

You have graciously gifted me this life. I often don't take the time to see the beauty in it. I walk right past all Your incredible creations and don't see Your hand. My thoughts think the worst. My perception and attitude are skewed toward negative, ugly thinking. Holy Spirit, I fall on my knees and beg You to help me change this about myself. I want to see the magnificence of Your creation. I want to appreciate the many gifts You've abundantly showered on me. I feel such shame for not being thankful for all that I have. Forgive me, Father.

God, thank you for fully loving me. You see me in the light of the being that You created in Your perfect image. When You look at me, You don't see all my bad decisions or my bad attitude. You have forgiven me, so You see my perfect soul that You created. How incredible! You love each and every part of me, even what I think is ugly or imperfect. Help me to see others in the perfect light as You see them. God Your love endures forever; let me shine Your light and reflect Your love in every interaction I have today. Let Your peace rule my heart.

LORD, help me to accept and appreciate my life as it is now. If there are any decisions I have made that I am not fully accepting, please assist me in embracing what is mine. I may not be where I ultimately want to be, but I know I need to find joy in You regardless of where I am. I invite You and Your Spirit to be present in all my situations and decisions. God, Your plan for my life is more than I could ever dream for, so please direct me toward the path to my purpose.

My choices have led me to my today. I'm choosing to be thankful for all my yesterdays, as they have been a gift and have shaped who I am. Whatever I choose to do today, I will choose to be thankful, for my thoughts and perception will decide my tomorrow. Spirit, help me to shape my tomorrow with peace, love, thankfulness, and all things good.

God, thank you for listening to me. Thank you for forgiving and always loving me. Thank you for Your constant presence and for the power of Your grace to assist me in being more of who I was made to be. I ask You to be at the center of my life as I move throughout this day. As always, let Your angels watch over my family and me, keeping us safe. Let Your kingdom come; let Your will be done.

Amen,

Your Humbled Child

PROBLEMS + CHALLENGES are gifted SO THAT you can OVERCOME them

Day 9:
Purpose for the Fight

*W*e tend to avoid problems at all cost, but surprisingly, some of our largest trials (such as dealing with a major attitude problem) serve us greatly. Their purpose in life is much larger than one would think. In the chapter "Finding Opportunity in the Challenge," we discussed how problems develop your character. Today, we will dig a bit deeper into their purpose.

How do you view problems? Do you despise them, or do you try to see the purpose through the difficulty? If you tend to look for the reason, then you're on the right track. Let's analyze this pesky attitude problem. You may feel as if it's really not that big of deal; after all, it's just "who you are." You may feel like you really don't have control over your attitude, so you haven't really tried to change. Maybe you have tried to overcome this problem before but have been left feeling defeated. Wherever you are on this journey, it's okay. Right here, right now, you are actively taking the step to change, and that's what matters. This challenge is here for a reason. The fact you're reading this book today is part of your plan. All problems that we face can be used for good.

Problems and challenges can actually be viewed as gifts. They give you the opportunity to overcome them, to grow and to learn, and to become a better person with a wider perspective. God certainly has a hand in the problems you face. Please don't misinterpret this! Know that God does not cause bad things to happen; the rain falls on the good and the bad in this world (Matthew 5:45), so don't let this discourage you! What He does is provide the opportunity, strength, motivation, comfort, and courage to work through the bad to achieve good out of any situation. Keep in mind, His focus is on your character development, not your comfort. Even so, you can be certain Jesus will provide you with a great reward once you've achieved this hurdle of overcoming a negative attitude.

Ephesians 3:9 explains to us that God is often mysterious in His ways. He has plans for us that, at times, we will not understand. Jesus explained to His disciples in John 16:20-22 how they would mourn over what would happen to Him. Imagine the loss and confusion they felt when Jesus died, but once they saw him three days later and experienced God's beautiful plan, their grief suddenly turned to joy. Challenges in your life are like this. It's hard in the struggle, but once you get through it and see the whole story, more joy exists than before.

Throughout life, we are constantly provided opportunities to learn and grow. You have been designed to face this specific problem and to solve it, not to avoid it or to escape it. Challenges in life will continue to surface in different ways in order to provide you the opportunity to learn the lesson. If you attempt to run, you will be presented with the same lesson to learn in a different way. Unfortunately, if you refuse to change, your life could be riddled with difficulties. It is here where the unlearned opportunities start to stack up on top of each other and become overwhelming. At that point, seeing the purpose in the struggle becomes nearly impossible. So step back and examine your hardships. What are they trying to teach you? Look for the ones that are giving you a chance to fix your negative attitude. You can and will experience and understand God's beautiful plan for your life; you only need to accept the challenge. This is the attitude antidote.

Problems and challenges are gifted to you so that you may overcome them.

Mysterious Father,

You are so great to bless me with all the good and challenging parts in my life. Bless me with faith to see problems through Your eyes, LORD, so I may not be discouraged. It is so amazing that You work all things for good for those that love You. And I love You, LORD, so I trust that You have gifted me all of my difficulties. But God, when I'm struggling, open my eyes to see the real purpose of my issues. Let Your light shine on the lessons I need to learn.

Father, in the depths of my struggles, my vision is clouded. It is murky, and I'm not thankful for the hurt I have to go through. It is here that I cry out to You for help! Carry me, heavenly Father, on Your shoulders. Lift me up, and give me hope. Without Your hope, I have nothing. Without You, I have nothing. Savior, forgive me for the times I have not seen Your hand or have blatantly chosen to ignore it.

I pray for a miracle: that I learn how to have a good attitude despite my circumstances. I trust in You and believe that You are an all-powerful, mighty God who preforms miracles daily. Today, I ask that I be Your miracle. Help me change and learn and grow so I may become a better and happier version of myself. I graciously ask that You assist me in the process of my personal growth.

You are my source of hope. I pray that You will fill me completely with joy and peace because I trust You. Through the power of the Holy Spirit, I will overflow with confident hope.

God, thank you for listening to me. Thank you for forgiving and always loving me. Thank you for Your constant presence and for the power of Your grace to assist me in being more of who I was made to be. I ask You to be at the center of my life as I move throughout this day. As always, let Your angels watch over my family and me, keeping us safe. Let Your kingdom come; let Your will be done.

Amen,

Your Humbled Child

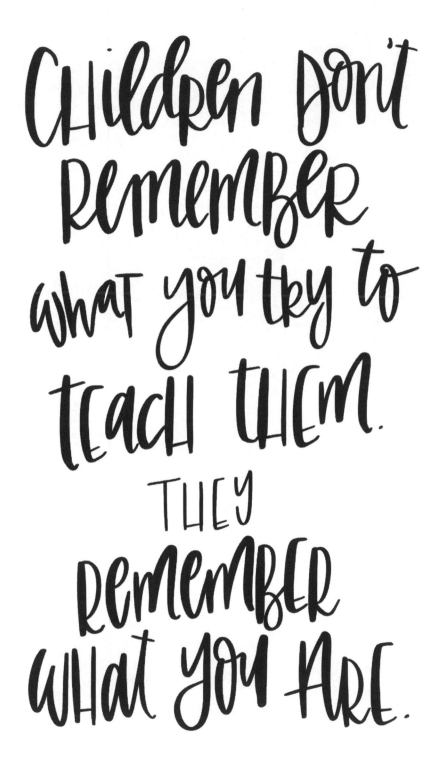

Children don't REMEMBER what you try to teach them. They REMEMBER what you are.

Day 10:
Your Powerful Role

"Direct your children onto the right path, and when they are older, they will not leave it." (Proverbs 22:6)

Whether you are empty nesters, a new parent, recently married, or finding your way through your early 20s, you play an important role in your family. Throughout your life, there may have been times when you've felt unimportant or even unloved. As the pendulum shifted, other times may have left you feeling completely overwhelmed with demand. Wherever you are in your journey, you are a very powerful person in your family's dynamic. This is especially true when raising children. Today's devotion is geared toward those who have children. But please take this to heart even if you don't have kids—you may be touched by the Holy Spirit in a surprising way.

"Care for the flock that God has entrusted to you. Watch over it willingly, not grudgingly—not for what you will get out of it, but because you are eager to serve God." (1 Peter 5:2)

As a parent, on a daily basis, your demeanor will shape who your children are, no matter their age. Jim Henson said, "The attitude that you have as a parent is what your kids will learn from, more than what you tell them. They don't remember what you try to teach them. They remember what you are."[1]

No one will disagree that parenting is tough. Each stage of a child's life brings beautiful blessings but also major

---

[1] https://www.goodreads.com/author/quotes/4427.Jim_Henson

challenges. At the end of a long day, our largest gift can often seem like our biggest nuisance. It is my humble opinion that the reason raising children is so difficult is because it provides an opportunity for us as parents to grow and mature. To raise them up well, they constantly require your self-sacrifice, patience, kindness, understanding, love, gentleness, and joy (the fruit of the Spirit of Galatians 5:22-23). There is nothing else in this world that allows for this much personal growth. So when it's tough, remember this little bit of insight.

Sometimes it may feel like you have "to fake it to make it" through the day because you're emotionally exhausted. And sometimes, you may not even be able to swing being fake. At times, we have all lost our self-control and have been a little too real with our negative feelings. The question is how often are you allowing yourself to lose control? My guess is that since attitude control is a challenge, this, too, may be something to work on, as the keys to fixing both problems are the same.

The best news of all is that changing your character through Christ to be a genuine, loving, even-keeled parent will also mean you're actively working on improving your overall attitude. By taking this journey of self-improvement, you're doing the BEST thing you can do for yourself and your family!

To illustrate this, take Kevin's story to heart. On Saturday mornings, Kevin watches his two young boys while his wife goes to the gym. Things were going smoothly until out of nowhere a temper tantrum erupted. The situation escalated, and Kevin's temper flared when his two boys began screaming and throwing things across the room. Suddenly, his attitude took hold and his tone quickly changed to convey his annoyance and anger. After shouting at his eldest son to go to his room, he soon realized he could have better handled the situation. When he went to talk with him, he first hugged the boy and then apologized for not controlling his own attitude or temper. He explained how he, as a dad, struggles with his attitude but that he's working on it every day.

Sadly, if you are tempted with a negative attitude, your children likely will face the same challenge. Choosing to be mature and meet the trial head-on will impart the greatest lesson to your children, no matter their age.

Don't be ashamed of your challenges. Open up to your family, and share with them how you're working on those struggles. Being transparent and showing your family the emotional growth you are achieving throughout this journey will be life-changing. This is the attitude antidote. Why? Because, in so doing, you will provide an excellent example for your family to follow in many ways. Everyone has weaknesses and personal flaws they need to work on, so openly convey that vulnerability expressed in a safe place is healthy behavior. It also teaches how to take responsibility for attitudes, actions, and self-improvement.

These principles don't stop with your children. Next time an argument sparks a sour disposition toward your spouse, quickly explain what upset you and ask for forgiveness. Discuss how you are taking steps to change, and share a point from your devotional. Chatting about how you are taking steps to change for your relationship will pay off in dividends! You will be amazed!

They don't remember what you try to teach them. They remember what you are.

Dear God,

You have blessed me with the most beautiful family. I greatly desire to lead my children on the right path, so I pray for Your Holy Spirit to work through me to raise my children in a Christ-like manner. Assist me in being the best parent I can be to the sweet souls that You have placed in my life. Thank you for trusting me with something so precious. Protector, please hold my children in Your hands and don't let them go.

With a heavy heart, I confess that I haven't cherished the biggest blessing of my life. I grow irritated. I become angry. I often speak to my family with a poor attitude and put myself before them. Oh God, please forgive this awful transgression. If one of them were taken from me, I would die inside. Spirit, I need Your help to match my true feelings toward my family with how I act and treat them. I need You daily. I need You hourly. Don't give up on me.

Creator, You have placed me in this family. I am here with my spouse, children, parents, and siblings for a reason. You have divinely designed our family to be together. Where there are any quarrels, contempt, or distance between us, please come in and soften hearts. LORD, open my eyes to see how my place in this family is important.

Jesus, You are the leader of my heart. Let the perfect life You led inspire me to be a better leader for my family. LORD, one day I will face the time when my life is coming to a close. I pray that I can look back at my life and feel good about how I treated the people I loved the most. I hope, when I look at myself, that I see a person who grew to overcome obstacles and was in control of her emotions and attitude. I want my life to be a shining light for You. Spirit, fill my head, heart, and soul. I pray for a remarkable transformation from an immature child to a mature adult who knows how to lead a family and to be a powerful guiding light for others.

God, thank you for listening to me. Thank you for forgiving and always loving me. Thank you for Your constant presence and for

the power of Your grace to assist me in being more of who I was made to be. I ask You to be at the center of my life as I move throughout this day. As always, let Your angels watch over my family and me, keeping us safe. Let Your kingdom come; let Your will be done.

Amen,

Your Humbled Child

your Attitude REFLECTS HOW you RECEIVE your gifts from God

Day 11:
The Spirit's Gifts

O ur marriages, children, parents, friends, work, possessions—even challenges—are all gifts from God. We have a whole lot to be thankful for! Let's read this next sentence slowly and let it really sink in. Our attitude reflects how we receive those gifts. Remember, God the Giver, sees our mind and heart's true feelings. If we say we're thankful but then continue on with a negative attitude, our words and actions aren't synonymous. Regardless of whether people or things fulfill our expectations or let us down, we should model Christ's example by respecting our gifts for what they are and what they could be.

Whenever you feel let down due to unfulfilled expectations, don't focus on the pain, for it is magnified by the evil one. He attempts to make hurt and discontentment shadow over the good. Look for the joy and meaning hiding in each life experience. Make it a daily practice to see the beauty and the good in all things and all people—despite irritations. If your eyes are open and your intentions are set, your perspective and attitude will change in response to disappointment.

We are given God's Spirit to help us here on earth to keep our hearts, souls, and minds aligned with our heavenly Creator. Ask and allow the Holy Spirit to guide your life so you will have a fighting chance to win against your sinful human nature. When you let the Spirit control your mind, you will be led to a life filled with peace. Accepting and focusing on the Spirit will make it easier to have a good attitude and to carry out your good intentions. Thankfully, "…you are not controlled by your sinful nature. You are controlled by the

Spirit if you have the Spirit of God living in you." (Romans 8:9a)

I highly encourage you to pause and read the fifth chapter of Galatians right now. It is worth reading in full, as it explains how we constantly fight our sinful nature that wants to fraternize with evil, meaning that we naturally crave sexual impurity, overdoing it at parties, lusting, hostility, quarreling, jealousy, acting out on anger, selfish ambition, and nursing a bad attitude. This natural drive toward harmful behavior is at constant battle with what the Spirit wants for us. To fight your natural tendencies, continuously keep your mind focused on developing the gifts given to you by the Spirit.

"But the Holy Spirit produces this kind of fruit in our lives: love, joy, peace, patience, kindness, goodness, faithfulness, gentleness, and self-control." (Galatians 5:22-23a)

Inviting the Holy Spirit into your life is the answer to fixing a bad attitude! Isn't it amazing how the Bible contains so much practical life advice completely applicable to our lives today? If we are left to our own devices, we are pulled toward that which is evil. If, however, we allow the Holy Spirit into our minds, hearts, and lives, we can truly change for the good. So, invite Him into your home. Say a prayer and send an invitation each day. He will gladly join you and produce in you His fruit. For His gifts listed in Galatians 5:22-23 are the attitude antidotes.

Focusing your thoughts on these good traits will, without a doubt, change you from the inside. You are capable of transforming into a person who radiates goodness and love and reacts with compassion and patience. When these traits are put into action, you can eradicate a negative outlook and attitude from your life. Philippians 1 contains a prayer written by Paul that I will personally pray for you each day to help you in your character transformation.

"I pray that your love will overflow more and more, and that you will keep on growing in knowledge and understanding. For I want you to understand what really matters, so that you may live pure and blameless lives until the day of Christ's return. May you always be filled with the fruit of your salvation—the righteous character produced in your life by Jesus Christ—for this will bring much glory and praise to God." (Philippians 1:9-11)

Your attitude reflects how you receive God's gifts.

Wonderful Father and Mighty God,

You have given me such a beautiful, abundant life. For all of my blessings, I am eternally thankful. My Giver, I humble myself in Your presence. I have not shown You thankfulness in response to my gifts. I am often irritated and don't appreciate what I have. When I stop to think about if it were all to be lost, I'm convicted. I am ashamed of my petty thoughts, attitudes, and actions. When I clear my perspective, I can see how much You've showered on me. Please forgive me for taking all that I have for granted.

My God, You have given me the greatest gift here on earth to help me through my challenges and to celebrate in my achievements. I am so thankful to be in the presence of Your Holy Spirit. Spirit, I invite You into my life today and tomorrow. Please fill my home with Your presence. Fill my head to transform my thoughts. Fill my heart to soften it. Fill my soul so I may feel You and Your life-giving presence. I will, with Your help, be able to live today from a thankful perspective.

Holy Spirit, God's Word says that You will produce in me everything that I need to overcome my attitude. Love, joy, peace, patience, kindness, goodness, faithfulness, gentleness, and self-control can be cultivated in me because of You! Please fill me and develop these wonderful attributes that I long for. Please make me into a person that is known for godly character.

I will overcome my sinful nature and attitude today with You. I am doomed for failure without You, Spirit. I need You. God, I am in awe that You care for me so much that You would give me such a Helper in this life. Spirit, overwhelm me and overwhelm my soul with Your presence so I may know You and God's astounding love. Let the fruit of the Spirit grow within me. Let me experience love, joy, peace, patience, kindness, goodness, faithfulness, gentleness, and self-control today and always.

God, thank you for listening to me. Thank you for forgiving and always loving me. Thank you for Your constant presence and for

the power of Your grace to assist me in being more of who I was made to be. I ask You to be at the center of my life as I move throughout this day. As always, let Your angels watch over my family and me, keeping us safe. Let Your kingdom come; let Your will be done.

Amen,

Your Humbled Child

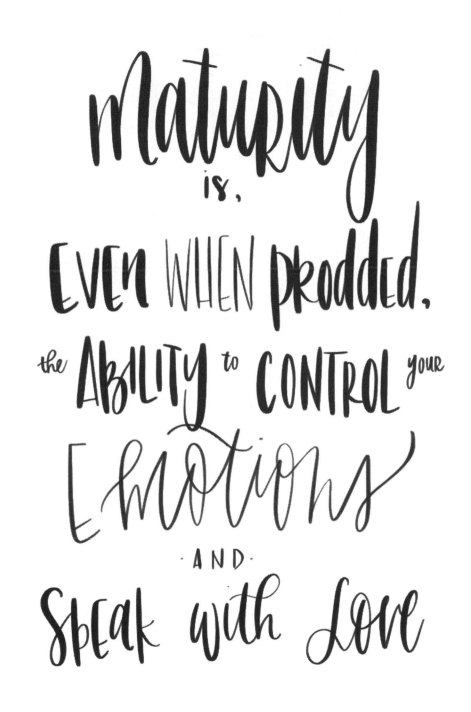

Maturity is,
even when prodded,
the ability to control your
Emotions
· and ·
speak with Love

Day 12:
Manifested Emotions

There's a difference between having prudent and kind honesty, and spilling out all our feelings over everything and everyone. The right time, place, and situation all must be taken into account. There is "...a time to be quiet and a time to speak" (Ecclesiastes 3:7). Whenever we're irritated, upset, or angry and ready to explode with a poor attitude is the exact time to keep silent! The best time to speak should come when emotions are cool, calm, and under control. I want to warn you that this chapter may be a bit hard to read, but it's necessary to review ourselves and our actions in real light so we may identify areas where growth is needed.

There are a great deal of verses in the Bible (especially in Proverbs) that explain how valuable it is to bite our tongues. If we're unable to control what comes out of our mouths, we are fools. It's a harsh reality, but it's what the Bible teaches. Over and over again, we learn that a wise man keeps silent. A wise man doesn't jump into quarrels. A wise man is able to, even when prodded, control his emotions and speak with love. This is our ultimate goal. Accepting this and putting it into practice is the attitude antidote.

I'm guessing if you struggle with your attitude, you also struggle with what you let come out of your mouth. They actually go hand in hand, as both of them have to do with the ability to control manifested emotions. It looks like this: Situations prompt thoughts, thoughts create emotions, and emotions are manifested into actions. This is the pipeline through which a negative attitude arises and your sense of control declines. Often, before you know it, you're irritated, slightly angry, and certainly quick to speak your mind. When negativity is allowed to flourish, the first stage is losing control of your emotions.

From here, it's so easy to let your mouth run wild. Thoughts you'd normally keep to yourself seem to leak out your mouth like water. "Fools have no interest in understanding; they only want to air their own opinions." (Proverbs 18:2) When your attitude has a hold of you, you already have decided to travel down the path of fools. It's a damning reality, but it's so true.

Proverbs warns of how important preventing a negative attitude is, for once it develops, self-control is hard to come by, and biting your tongue is more challenging than ever before. Make it easy and commit yourself to working on attitude prevention, so staying in control is an easier task. You can do this. For where your mind, focus, and attention go, there also goes the opportunity to heal. Ask the Holy Spirit for help with this one daily (if not hourly, if you're really struggling).

It can be trying at times to always remain under control, especially when you feel as if you're being prodded from every direction and your cup is ready to overflow. In those moments, choose to change your train of thought. Instead of focusing on the struggle, shift your energy toward what you intend to do. Make a radical decision, and say multiple loving, kind, uplifting, and gentle statements aloud. Speak prayers out loud. If you're in touch with your body, you'll feel a strange kind of physical resistance in your being. This is good! Continue attempting to stimulate that resistance feeling until goodness overtakes evil and your hovering attitude is banished. "…Let everything you say be good and helpful, so that your words will be an encouragement to those who hear them." (Ephesians 4:29b)

"A truly wise person uses few words; a person with understanding is even-tempered. Even fools are thought wise when they keep silent; with their mouths shut, they seem intelligent." (Proverbs 17:27-28)

Even when prodded, maturity is the ability to control your emotions and speak with love.

LORD Jesus,

I cry out to You from the depths of my foolishness. I continually choose to walk the same path that leads me toward being the person I do not wish to be. My attitude gets in the way of me being a wise person, and because of that, I plead for Your forgiveness, and I'm asking for Your help.

You've warned me time and time again that a wise man holds his tongue and speaks with love. Sometimes I wonder how this is possible, as I struggle so. However, I am given hope when I look up to You. For I know You can and will change my heart if I only ask. So I am asking, Jesus, for Your transforming hand to mold me into a wiser person today.

Jesus, these are the instances when I need Your intervention. When I'm tired and want a break. When I'm hurt and need comforting. When I'm scared and need assurance. When I'm sick or hungry and need relief. When I'm lost and I don't know where to go. When I'm not happy with myself or the people in my life and need love. Looking at all these instances, I see that You are the answer to all my problems.

You are my help, Jesus! I lift up my eyes to the hills. Where does my help come from? My help comes from You, LORD, who made heaven and earth. You will not let me stumble; You watch over me and will not falter or slumber. You LORD are my keeper. You LORD will keep me from all harm and watch over my life. I trust You will keep watch over me as I come and go, both now and forevermore (Psalm 121).

All-knowing God, grant me knowledge so I may use words with restraint. Compassionate Father, grant me understanding so I may be even-tempered. Let everything I say be good and helpful, so that my words will be an encouragement to those who hear them. I want to understand the needs of others before airing my own opinion.

Jesus, save me from being a fool! Cultivate in me a heart of patience, kindness, goodness, faithfulness, and self-control. For only You—Father, Son, and Holy Ghost—can bless me like this. Thank you for hearing my prayers; I trust and believe that You hear me.

God, thank you for listening to me. Thank you for forgiving and always loving me. Thank you for Your constant presence and for the power of Your grace to assist me in being more of who I was made to be. I ask You to be at the center of my life as I move throughout this day. As always, let Your angels watch over my family and me, keeping us safe. Let Your kingdom come; let Your will be done.

Amen,

Your Humbled Child

self control requires sacrifice.

Day 13:
Self-Control

"For God has not given us a spirit of fear and timidity, but of power, love, and self-discipline." (2 Timothy 1:7)

"God blesses those who work for peace, for they will be called the children of God." (Matthew 5:9)

Self-control is the ultimate answer to any negative attitude. As we've learned already, self-control is a gift that comes from the Holy Spirit. It's quite simple, really: To get rid of, or prevent, a bad attitude, self-control is the first line of defense. It means doing the right thing when it feels hard. There is no self-control without sacrifice. Without it, we have no fighting chance against giving into our natural tendencies. Figuring out how to exercise our own self-control is how we will create the change we're seeking. Rest assured, the answer may be easier than you think.

Second Timothy 1:3-9 explains how through knowing Him, God has given us everything we need to live a godly life. Because of His glory and excellence, He has given us the ability to escape the world's corruption caused by human desires. We are called to supplement our faith with moral excellence, knowledge, self-control, patient endurance, godliness, and with love and affection for everyone. We are then told the more we are able to grow in attributes like these, the more productive and useful we'll be.

It comes down to this question: Do you want to be changed and to live for God? It's a difficult but real decision we all must make. Either we choose to live for ourselves, or we choose to make sacrifices and to live for God's glory. There really are no other options.

Examine yourself and find what is motivating you to change your attitude. Is it to improve your relationships? To feel better about yourself? Or is it to obey God? Hopefully, the answer is all of the above with an emphasis on the latter. When you make someone other than Jesus the reason to change, eventually they will let you down. And then, where does the motivation go? To be in complete control of yourself and your attitude, your motivation must remain in pleasing and obeying God. Only then can you be completely successful in becoming a person who has a loving, patient, and kind attitude even in the midst of struggle.

The answer lies with Jesus. Make Him your motivation, and you will become who you want to be. This is the attitude antidote. He will help you achieve self-control, which will offer the strength you need to succeed.

"So then, since Christ suffered physical pain, you must arm yourselves with the same attitude he had...You won't spend the rest of your lives chasing your own desires, but you will be anxious to do the will of God." (1 Peter 4:1-2)

Jesus made the ultimate sacrifice for you and for everyone who chooses to believe and accept His gift of grace. There is no greater love that has ever been displayed. Keeping this fact in the forefront of your mind on a daily basis will help you maintain proper perspective. Jesus suffered so much because He loves you! What motivation! He deserves everything, so perhaps controlling your attitude doesn't seem like such a challenge after all.

"Always be full of joy in the LORD. I say it again— rejoice! Let everyone see that you are considerate in all you do. Remember, the LORD is coming soon." (Philippians 4:4-5)

There is no self-control without sacrifice.

Heavenly Father, Jesus Christ, and Blessed Spirit,

I fall to my knees in awe of You. The sacrifices You've made on my behalf are jaw-dropping. My breath is taken away when I meditate on all the goodness You possess and shower onto me. When I think of why You do so much for me, I don't know. All I know from Your word is that You are a God of love. You chose to suffer on my behalf so I may live with You in a perfect eternity. Words of gratitude cannot express how humbled I feel in Your presence.

Since my praise isn't enough, I choose to give You my life. Because of You and Your grace, I have a motivator unlike any here on earth. My motivation comes from You, LORD. Your steadfast love, acceptance, and forgiveness make me want to change. Let Your Spirit guide my life in being a person You would be proud to call Yours. It is my job as a child of Yours to begin acting as if I'm part of Your family. Grant me self-control, for my natural tendency is to lose it.

Jesus, even when You were being tortured, mocked, and ridiculed, You continued to love and remain in control. Spirit, help paint this picture in my mind as a constant reminder and motivation to endure whatever it is I am feeling fritzed about. I still struggle, although what I deal with and what You've endured aren't comparable in the least. My human nature often takes over, and my vision becomes clouded. I lose sight of anything but myself. When I turn inward and let myself become flooded with negative emotion, please reach out Your hand so I may pull myself out quickly.

LORD, help me grow; I accept my challenges as fuel to improve myself. You have given me everything I need to live a godly life here. Help me use those gifts for good. Let the fruit of the Spirit grow in me so others may see love, joy, peace, patience, kindness, goodness, faithfulness, gentleness, and self-control. I invite You in, Holy Spirit, to be the farmer of goodness in my heart. God, Your saving kindness guides me toward living with self-control.

God, thank you for listening to me. Thank you for forgiving and always loving me. Thank you for Your constant presence and for

the power of Your grace to assist me in being more of who I was made to be. I ask You to be at the center of my life as I move throughout this day. As always, let Your angels watch over my family and me, keeping us safe. Let Your kingdom come; let Your will be done.

Amen,

Your Humbled Child

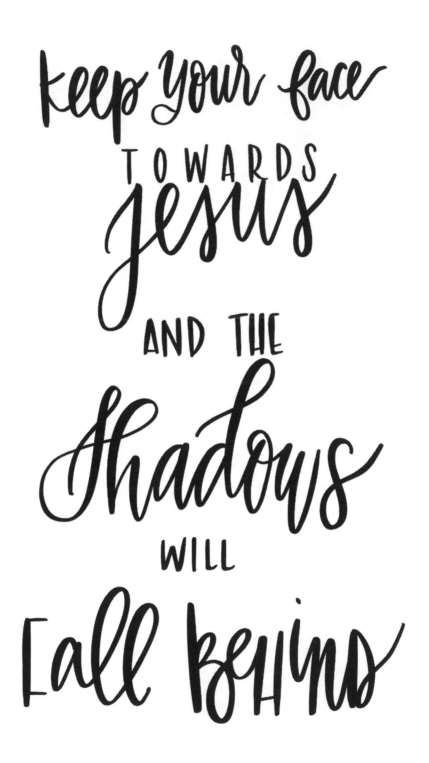

keep your face TOWARDS jesus AND THE Shadows WILL Fall behind

Day 14:
Attitude of Christ

"Is there any encouragement from belonging to
Christ? Any comfort from his love? Any fellowship
together in the Spirit? Are your hearts tender and
compassionate? Then make me truly happy by
agreeing wholeheartedly with each other, loving one
another, and working together with one mind and
purpose. Don't be selfish; don't try to impress others.
Be humble, thinking of others as better than
yourselves. Don't look out only for your own interests,
but take an interest in others, too. You must have the
same attitude that Christ Jesus had. Though he was
God, he did not think of equality with God as
something to cling to. Instead, he gave up his divine
privileges; he took the humble position of a slave and
was born as a human being. When he appeared in
human form, he humbled himself in obedience to God
and died a criminal's death on a cross. Therefore, God
elevated him to the place of highest honor and gave
him the name above all other names, that at the name
of Jesus every knee should bow, in heaven and on
earth and under the earth, and every tongue declare
that Jesus Christ is LORD, to the glory of God the
Father." (Philippians 2:1-11)

This reading from the second chapter of Philippians is titled:
"Have the attitude of Christ." Since the focus of this
journey is to improve our attitudes, who better to model our
new selves after? This is why the verses are here for you to
read. Best to read, reread, and read them again. And then
tomorrow, read them again! Bookmark this page because
adopting Christ's attitude is the attitude antidote.

The second chapter of Philippians provides us with the
answers to correcting any attitude problem. I encourage you to

write down all 11 verses and to keep them with you always. Each day brings its own challenges, so every time you reread these verses, you may hear the Holy Spirit speaking to you in a different way. Highlight what speaks to you now, and focus on that today. Let's take a closer look at Philippians 2 and extract the lessons God has provided.

1. **Agree wholeheartedly with each other.** Bottom line: Don't pick a fight, don't be quarrelsome, and don't easily jump into a disagreement. Make it your goal to live in harmony with those around you. Become a peacemaker. Finding daily peace with the Spirit's help before the day begins will make it easier to follow this advice.

2. **Don't be selfish.** Google's definition of selfish is: "lacking consideration for others; concerned chiefly with one's own personal profit or pleasure." Be considerate, and consider the needs of others before your own. Remember, every single decision you make eventually adds up to equal something big: your character.

3. **Be humble.** Don't be overly proud, arrogant, or conceited. Being humble means to minimize your own importance. This goes against our worldly philosophy that we need to stand out from the crowd, proving our importance. A new challenge this generation has is handling social media with humbleness. Unfortunately, the number of "likes" we receive on social media provides a false sense of worth, and often our mood is affected by that counterfeit encouragement. Remember: Your worth comes from the LORD, the one who made you and has given you the gracious gift of forgiveness. It is not from the reassurance that you are adored by the world. And most of all, humble yourself in the sight of the LORD.

4. **Take an interest in others.** Jesus's entire life was about serving other people. This gives us insight into what is really important. Hectic schedules make this challenging to carry out, but if you start to slow down your daily routine, incorporating this principle can be achieved easily. Take an extra minute and talk to others you are in contact with—cashiers, people in line, waiters, anyone, and everyone. Offer them a compliment, make eye contact and smile, and take the time to be cordial and not rushed. Life is about connecting with people and being a shining light for Jesus. Allow others to see that light burn.

5. **Obey and give glory to God.** Basic advice, right?! Learn God's rules for your life, and follow them. Do unto your neighbor as yourself. Connect daily with Your Heavenly Father. This will give glory to God.

Jesus has given the ultimate instruction to transform yourself and your attitude. If you focus on these five pieces of advice, you will no longer have an attitude problem. Instead, you will have a life modeled after Him.

Keep your face towards Jesus, and the shadows will fall behind you.

Jesus,

How I long to have an attitude like Yours! I receive such encouragement and comfort from belonging to You. I pray that You soften my heart, making me, my words, and my reactions tender and compassionate. Thank you for being born human, for giving up Your divine privileges and for humbling Yourself. You gave Yourself as a living sacrifice for me. For that, I am eternally in debt to Your awesome acts of love. Your life was an inspiration to teach me how to live with intention.

Jesus, I dedicate myself today to model my life after You. Heavenly Father, I pray that You will help me to truly agree wholeheartedly with others. Spirit, I need Your help to be a peacemaker. Please forgive me for often having the desire to be quarrelsome. I know this is not Your will for me. Prince of Peace, please fill my life and relationships with Your peaceful presence that spreads to everyone around me.

Being selfish is something that comes very naturally. Please forgive each and every time I have put myself and my wants before others. LORD, my character is at stake here. I need You to make me into the person I was meant to be.

Jesus, Your life was the most humbling experience anyone has ever gone through. You went from being God to being man and dying like a criminal. I need Your wisdom to become humble. I often get reassurance and feelings of worth from things of this world when I know that being Your child is where my worth comes from. Help me to remember this today.

Jesus, Your life was all about serving others. Please teach me how to be a servant and take interest in those around me. I'm sorry for often dismissing others that You love just as much as me. Forgive my arrogance, my selfishness, and my sinful nature.

At the name of You, Jesus, every knee shall bow. Jesus Christ, You are LORD, glory to God the Father.

God, thank you for listening to me. Thank you for forgiving and always loving me. Thank you for Your constant presence and for the power of Your grace to assist me in being more of who I was made to be. I ask You to be at the center of my life as I move throughout this day. As always, let Your angels watch over my family and me, keeping us safe. Let Your kingdom come; let Your will be done.

Amen,

Your Humbled Child

GRACE
is an
undeserved
gift

Day 15:
Reacting with Grace and Mercy

What triggers your attitude? It's likely there are a handful of things that tend to get under your skin on a regular basis. So, today take some time to identify those main triggers and write them down. This is a very important step in prevention because wherever negativity is allowed to form, chaos lurks. When emotions run high and your patience is cut short, it's hard to reverse the pattern of giving into negative feelings and emotions. Bottom line: A plan is needed before a trigger occurs. If you can identify the situation and anticipate the feelings that precede the attitude struggle, it makes it easier to choose a better reaction.

I have learned one of my biggest triggers for a poor attitude is when my husband comes into the room with his own bad mood. Of course, this is not totally a surprise, as we've already touched on how the emotions of others can quickly transfer like a rampant disease. This definitely plays a part, but there is more to my temptation. When I am spoken to with a condescending tone, it sets me off. After all, in my mind, I don't deserve to be spoken to like that. Plus, I tend to become overly irritated when the energy of the room downshifts. My brain pattern history triggers a spiral into the same condescending tone, and I spit it right back to my husband. It is like a subconscious need to repay him eye-for-an-eye.

Using my example, let's take all the principles we've discussed to create a plan to avoid this negative pattern in the future. First, I've identified that his bad mood is a trigger. I will use this knowledge as an indicator the next time I see him coming in with negativity. Even before he speaks, I will be able to recognize his frame of mind because of his body language and facial expression. I will need to mentally prepare myself to fight my natural response.

Second, I will pray a silent prayer immediately for self-control, gentleness, and understanding. I need to have sympathy for my husband and to seek to help him instead of caring only about my own needs. I need to be willing to self-sacrifice and shift the focus toward helping him.

Third, I will focus on applying the fruit of the Spirit to care for someone beyond myself. Most of all, I must remember to love. When we were married, I chose to love him in good and in bad. And even though he won't be bringing anything good to the room at that particular moment, I will need to react to his attitude with grace and mercy. He may not deserve it at that time, but I must look past that and react for the greater good of him and our marriage.

Our ultimate goal is to react to others with grace and mercy. But what exactly does that mean? In its simplest form, grace is an undeserved gift. Mercy means that a deserved punishment is not given. Ponder these two words for a minute, and let their definitions sink into your soul, for this is the attitude antidote.

"But God is so rich in mercy, and he loved us so much, that even though we were dead because of our sins, he gave us life when he raised Christ from the dead. (It is only by God's grace that you have been saved!)" (Ephesians 2:4-5)

If we choose to react with grace and mercy, we will be serving God and obeying Him, which is even further motivation. Jesus has commanded us to love like He did in every situation. Especially at first, you may seriously struggle in the moment to change and offer grace and mercy. The only way to overcome this is to make your reason to change about Jesus. Lean on Him; He is your only help, and He is worth it.

I encourage you to put an action plan into place for your biggest triggers. Plan how you can transform your typical reaction with the help of the Spirit and Jesus's love. The LORD told Paul, "My grace is all you need. My power works best in weakness." (2 Corinthians 12:9a)

Grace is an undeserved gift.

Jesus,

> *Your life has painted a picture of perfect grace and mercy. Your perfect, all-consuming love has shown us what grace and mercy truly mean. They require sacrifice of myself, just as You showed when You took on the sins of the world. Though You were a perfect person, You suffered an indescribable death that I deserved. Thank you for bearing my punishment and for showing me the meaning of mercy.*

> *Jesus, when I give into my attitude, it really comes down me choosing myself over others, including You. I struggle with having self-control and showing others love, grace, and mercy. Help me in the moment to see that You are God, You are the judge, and I don't need to play that role.*

> *It is my job to love as You did, Jesus, so please forgive my failed attempts. I humbly ask for Your wisdom, vision, and energy to make loving choices. Holy Spirit, please convict my heart in the very moment I need You. Carry me through this personal change, for I cannot do this without You.*

> *I will keep You as my motivation because You truly deserve it, and my family and friends deserve it, too! I have chosen to place my selfish desires over them so many times, and I am so ashamed. Forgive me, Father, for when my tree bears no fruit. From the depths of my soul, I aspire to be a person who is known for my loving actions and reactions. Please help me in changing myself and my heart.*

> *You have said that Your grace is all I need and that it works best in my weakness. LORD, I am weak, and I am reaching out to You. I need Your grace and mercy. Help me show this virtue to others in all situations. When I am afraid, I will put my trust in You. I lift my eyes up to the hills—where does my help come from? My help comes from You, LORD, Maker of heaven and earth.*

> *God, thank you for listening to me. Thank you for forgiving and always loving me. Thank you for Your constant presence and for*

the power of Your grace to assist me in being more of who I was made to be. I ask You to be at the center of my life as I move throughout this day. As always, let Your angels watch over my family and me, keeping us safe. Let Your kingdom come; let Your will be done.

Amen,

Your Humbled Child

BE QUICK to LISTEN slow to SPEAK slow to get ANGRY

JAMES 1:19

Day 16:
Anger

Anger means something different for each person. Something that upset us last week may not have the same effect this week due to current feelings and circumstances. But one thing is constant: Anger almost always sparks a negative attitude.

Just to be clear, anger in and of itself is not a sin. The Bible describes multiple times how Jesus openly displayed anger. In Matthew 21, Jesus walked into a busy temple and intentionally knocked over tables of merchants selling animals for sacrifice and then made whips of rope (John 2:15) to drive them out! He was infuriated because they were taking advantage of people in a holy place. The bottom line was that Jesus felt angry—but for a noble cause.

However, the most notable thing to me is that right after this big scene, he didn't storm out. He didn't stew and discuss how wretched the merchants were with friends. Instead, he turned around and gently healed the blind and the lame. Jesus's example here is an incredible lesson, for it teaches us to continue loving right after an upset instead of wallowing in our anger.

So let's review and bring some real-world examples into these lessons. Jesus showed us that our ultimate goal is to only experience anger for honorable causes, quickly letting it go and moving forward in love. Unfortunately for us, anger sparks all too often. Life in general frequently rubs us the wrong way. Being aware of this, we must identify what "pushes our buttons," so to speak.

Make yourself aware of when, with whom, and what causes you to lose your cool. Becoming aware of your triggers is critical to avoid becoming angry over something mundane just to have it lead to an ongoing negative attitude. You may have a difficult time in the morning when the kids need to get ready for school. Or, perhaps, you grow frustrated when your spouse comes in from work and immediately sits on the couch and pulls out the phone. Maybe it's a coworker who ruffles your feathers. When reviewing your triggers, identify your biggest annoyances and put a plan in place to lengthen your patience string. Being aware will prevent anger from blindsiding you. This is only the first step. From here, you must choose your reactions to others wisely. Pray a silent prayer when you feel like anger may be creeping in, and keep Jesus's example close to your heart.

Emily knows she has a very short string of patience when 5:00 p.m. hits and she needs to fix dinner. The minute she walks in from work, it begins. Like clockwork, the kids begin whining for a snack, complaining about each other, and quarreling. The dogs underfoot remind her that they haven't been fed. The baby is nonstop climbing up her leg so she can't move. It's understandable that a perfect storm like this one would lead Emily to her breaking point. Knowing this, she takes preventative measures to ease the 5:00 p.m. rush hour. Before the chaos begins, she feeds the dogs early, utilizes the TV to distract the children, and sits the baby in the highchair with a handful of cereal to munch and an activity to follow. Most importantly, she recalls her commitment to not become easily angered, and she focuses her energy on her blessings and the LORD.

James 1:19-21 says, "Understand this, my dear brothers and sisters: You must all be quick to listen, slow to speak, and slow to get angry. Human anger does not produce the righteousness God desires. So get rid of all the filth and evil in your lives, and humbly accept the word God has planted in your hearts, for it has the power to save your souls."

We must be quick to listen, slow to speak, and slow to get angry. God gives us the answer right here. This is the attitude antidote. Taking the focus off your emotions and opening your ears will result in a healthier response. Listen to those around you, even if as in Emily's case, it's whining. For she can attempt to see the reason behind the whine. Possibly even more importantly, listen to yourself as you strive to improve. Listen to the Holy Spirit's quiet whisper telling you: "This too shall pass." Listen to and accept the peace that only Jesus can provide.

Once you give in to your feelings in a heated moment (even nonverbally), you open the door to allow anger to set in. Self-control is the answer, and the Holy Spirit is your ultimate help. So in the midst of any hard situation, immediately turn to God and pray a small prayer to help you keep control.

"...be quick to listen, slow to speak, and slow to get angry."
(James 1:19)

Jesus,

The glorious life You lived has shown me how I need to be living my life. Your perfect example gives me hope and a goal for excellence. LORD, I struggle in multiple areas, including controlling my anger. I often become upset over things I shouldn't. I let people and their actions determine my reactions and mood. I need Your Spirit to help me with my patience and self-control. Not only this, but when I do become angry, I don't easily let it go. My ugly nature wants to harbor and stew in hateful thoughts, attitudes, and actions. Jesus, I humble myself and ask that You forgive me.

God, I need self-control in the most basic way. I sometimes feel as if I don't have a choice how I act and, because of that, You are my only answer. May Your Word convict me! My anger does not produce the righteousness that You desire from me. LORD, show me how to be quick to listen and slow to speak.

Thank you for Your wise words in helping to guide my life. I know I struggle with my patience. I struggle with my response to the people I love. God, I struggle with becoming angry and letting that anger turn my soul ugly with attitude. I'm so sorry for hurting You and those around me who don't deserve that behavior.

LORD, the only way I can change is through the Holy Spirit and Your astounding grace. I humbly ask for Your power to come and change me from the inside out. Plant Your Word in my heart. I pray that the Holy Spirit helps me to accept and apply it to my life.

God, thank you for listening to me. Thank you for forgiving and always loving me. Thank you for Your constant presence and for the power of Your grace to assist me in being more of who I was made to be. I ask You to be at the center of my life as I move throughout this day. As always, let Your angels watch over my family and me, keeping us safe. Let Your kingdom come; let Your will be done.

Amen,

Your Humbled Child

Let go of your PRIDE IT'S NOT GIVING UP, it's growing up

Day 17:
Pride

"Because of the privilege and authority God has given me, I give each of you this warning: Don't think you are better than you really are. Be honest in your evaluation of yourselves, measuring yourselves by the faith God has given us. Just as our bodies have many parts and each part has a special function, so it is with Christ's body. We are many parts of one body, and we all belong to each other....Live in harmony with each other. Don't be too proud to enjoy the company of ordinary people. And don't think you know it all!" (Romans 12:3-5, 16)

Romans 12, which is titled "A Living Sacrifice to God," gives us incredible direction and wisdom for living a godly life. Twice it mentions to beware of thinking we're better than someone else, so we must work against our human nature to compare ourselves with one another. Why? It can lead us down a dark rabbit hole, where vision of what is good and right becomes clouded. Always remember that each of us has our own challenges to overcome, and each of us has our own lessons to learn. We mustn't grow prideful if we recognize that someone else hasn't yet mastered one area of life that we do not struggle with, for we certainly have our own battles to fight.

Pride is rampant in the world of work and education. Climbing the ladder is often a vicious game and doesn't leave too much room for the care and concern of others. Advancing through personal achievement is often a double-edged sword, because while we're eager to celebrate accomplishments, it easily lands us in a prideful spot. It's almost impossible not to judge others lower than us in rank or grade.

But Romans provides us with some valuable advice. We are warned to evaluate ourselves based on our faith, not our earthly titles. We are taught to recognize that each one of us has an important role to play in God's plan. While it may be one of the most difficult things to do at work or school, we must teach ourselves to value each person we come into contact with, regardless of job title, what they've achieved, or academic rank. We are all here to fulfill a larger purpose, and that's what is important. This is the attitude antidote.

But pride doesn't merely exist at work and school. I recently realized that I struggle quite a bit with pride at home. I was taken aback, as I never considered pride to be much of an issue. It dawned on me when a quarrel would arise with my husband. As many spouses do, I would always be firm in my stance and would rarely budge, thinking I was completely right. I would even justify my negative attitude, which would certainly bloom in the midst of the argument.

Society actually makes a joke out of this issue and even propagates acting with pride. Google "Woman is always right quote," and you'll be bombarded with them, like this one: "Marriage is a relationship in which one is always right and the other is the husband!" I realized a drastic change needed to occur if I wanted my marriage to last. According to God's Word, I needed to begin seeing things from my husband's point of view and to stop thinking that my side was superior to his; it was simply different. I needed to value his opinion and respect him although I disagreed. This meant no attitude, no fighting, no contempt, and no harsh thoughts or words.

Before parting today, let's touch on one last thought regarding the first verse quoted. "Don't be too proud to enjoy the company of ordinary people." Whether we are homeless or own seven homes, we are all God's children, and He equally loves us all. Simply put, we each have our own unique part to play, and no one is better than anyone else.

Let go of your pride. It's not giving up; it's growing up.

LORD Jesus,

How I have sinned against You and the people You love! I have hurt so many along the way without even knowing it. My prideful thoughts, attitudes, and actions that were once unrecognized have now convicted me to take a look at how I am treating the people in my community and at home.

God, I beg that You forgive my judgmental thoughts that have been part of my life for so long. I need Your grace daily, for I often don't even realize what harm I do. Let the thoughts in my head, the words of my mouth, and the tone of my voice convey love to all. I wish to have an attitude like You, Jesus. Spirit, convict my soul when I have crossed the line.

God I pray for each and every one of Your children. They all are part of Your miraculous creation and plan, and I am thankful to be part of it. For I am only a grain of sand on a beach that runs for miles and miles. I choose to humble myself in the sight of You, LORD. Spirit, humble me in the company of others. Open my eyes and heart to appreciate others and to see them for the wonderful people You have created them to be.

I struggle with my pride. Please teach me how to be pleased with my achievements without being overly prideful. Please teach me how to step back in an argument and see the other side. Creator, grant me a heart of flesh that is full of empathy. Jesus, teach me how to love like You did and how to see everyone through Your eyes.

God, thank you for listening to me. Thank you for forgiving and always loving me. Thank you for Your constant presence and for the power of Your grace to assist me in being more of who I was made to be. I ask You to be at the center of my life as I move throughout this day. As always, let Your angels watch over my family and me, keeping us safe. Let Your kingdom come; let Your will be done.

Amen,

Your Humbled Child

Forgiveness is not an act it's an Attitude

Day 18:
Your Past

It's true that our past experiences have shaped who we are today. Others greatly impact our lives—for the good and for the bad. Each of us has been wounded, let down, influenced, blessed, and cherished by at least one person in our lives. This is why it's so important to keep good company. First Corinthians 15:33 warns, "Bad company corrupts good character." Childhood experiences and relationships, especially, have a profound effect because while we are young, we are extremely moldable and easily influenced.

Surprisingly or maybe not surprisingly, our parents have much to do with the attitude we currently have today. Not only this, but they also have had a major influence on how happy, patient, loving, open, and forgiving we've been over the course of our lives. Regardless of who we've become, the choices we've made and continue to make are a reflection of how we grew up—for better or for worse. Take Brent's story, for example.

Brent grew up in a privileged family. His parents are still together, but since he can remember, they've been fighting or bickering about something. His dad was often stressed about work, and his mom was usually flustered or irritated. Overall, his childhood wasn't bad; he received everything he needed, and then some—but emotionally, he longed for more. Fast-forward 20 years, and Brent struggles with finding happiness in life. He has a bleak outlook, struggles with a short fuse, stresses out about everything, and often argues with coworkers and his wife. He feels empty, as if something is missing, and often wonders about the meaning of life.

From an outsider's perspective looking at the summary of Brent's life, it may be easy to see where his bad attitude and poor outlook on life originated from. Now, this isn't an opportunity to assign blame. It's a chance to see that possibly you've adopted some ugly characteristics throughout life from your parents or caretakers. It's an opportunity to accept responsibility for your own actions and to decide to change the parts about yourself that need a reset. It's an opportunity to let go of your past and to make a new future for yourself. You have the power to stop this negative generational pattern! But before you do that, you cannot skip a very important step.

If you have any memories that evoke feelings of hurt, disdain, resentment, or anger, realize that you're holding the past inside you. Don't take this lightly; remaining here is dangerous. When they are left untouched, feelings like these will eventually rot away your true self, your beauty, your purpose, and your happiness.

The most powerful healing tool available is forgiveness: forgiveness for the offender, the offense, and the feelings evoked. Whether the hurt comes from childhood experiences, your parents, a past relationship, friends, coworkers, or whoever it may be—let go, and forgive them for what they did. Not for their sakes, but for yours. Forgiveness is not an act; it's an attitude. Once you're able to let go of the past, you will be a new person. Your heavy heart can easily be healed and made new. You can readily forgive, let go, and transform who you are. Ask God for His healing and transforming power, and cast all your cares on Him. This is the attitude antidote.

Jesus spoke these words: "If you forgive those who sin against you, your heavenly Father will forgive you. But if you refuse to forgive others, your Father will not forgive your sins." (Matthew 6:14-15) Holding onto past hurts causes so much sorrow because, not only do you carry around the pain others have caused, but also your own unforgiving heart.

"Get rid of all bitterness, rage, anger, harsh words, and slander, as well as all types of evil behavior. Instead, be kind to each other, tenderhearted, forgiving one another, just as God through Christ has forgiven you." (Ephesians 4:31-32)

Forgiveness is not an act; it's an attitude.

Jesus,

Your entire purpose was fulfilled when You so selflessly died on my behalf. Your life was not only a living testament, but You also became the sacrifice for my sin. The fact that You so easily forgive me is such an inspiration. There is no hesitation, no anger—there is only love. Your love transcends all things and envelops me and my sin. You immediately forgive the hurt I cause You and others, if only I ask.

God, it's so hard to let go of the transgressions committed against me. Thank you for Your Word, which warns me that Your forgiveness will not be granted if I don't offer the same forgiveness as You do. Often, I've held onto hurt. Please help me to let it go as quickly as it comes.

Jesus Christ, my heavenly Savior, help me to forgive others. Heavenly Father, take my hardened heart and make it a heart of flesh, for You alone can help me. Each experience, memory, moment of hurt—let it be Yours. LORD, I know, it is not my place to judge others, even if it's at my expense. It is my job to love. So God, right now I choose to lighten my heart and to give You what I've been carrying with me for so long. Today I choose to love and forgive.

God, though others have helped shape who I am today, I take responsibility for my own actions and attitudes. Thank you for the people and experiences in my life. Thank you for the hard times, as well as the good times, as they have allowed me to grow. I want to be a happy, lighthearted individual who touches others with goodness. Jesus, now that I have forgiven others who have transgressed against me, I humbly ask for Your forgiveness. Redeemer, redeem my soul! Let me feel the freedom that is imminent because I have forgiven others and You have forgiven me.

God, thank you for listening to me. Thank you for forgiving and always loving me. Thank you for Your constant presence and for the power of Your grace to assist me in being more of who I was made to be. I ask You to be at the center of my life as I move throughout this day. As always, let Your angels watch over my family and me, keeping us safe. Let Your kingdom come; let Your will be done.

Amen,
Your Humbled Child

FEAR IS A LIAR

Day 19:
Fear and Worry

We all fear. We all worry. Fear and worry are two roses that bloom from the same stem. When something threatens our livelihood, happiness, health, or anything else of value, fear and worry set in. From this vantage point, it's almost impossible to see blessings, choose happiness, or transform a bad attitude, if one starts to form. Fear and worry work hand-in-hand like a storm, quickly bringing in dark rainclouds to cast over the sunshine. Their darkness spreads, forming a gloomy emptiness, making God's light seem so far away.

Know that fear and worry are not from God. They are from the evil one who attempts to guide us away from Jesus. There is an incredible song by Zach Williams that illustrates that fear is directly from Satan and to remember that he is a liar.[2] The song references how through fear, the enemy of your soul will attempt to take your very breath, stop you from following God, and destroy your peace. The devil is actively at work when we are anxious with fear and worry. His intention is to steal us away from Jesus and His peace.

Surprisingly, the very essence of worry is distrust. When we choose to let our minds become overwhelmed with negative thoughts and fear, we are choosing to not trust God. Instead, we give in to the devil and his ploy.

The LORD actually commands us to be strong and courageous because He is with us wherever we go. He spoke these words to Joshua after Moses died: "This is my

---

[2] Williams, Zach. *Chainbreaker*. Essential Music Publishing, 2016.

command—be strong and courageous! Do not be afraid or discouraged. For the LORD your God is with you wherever you go." (Joshua 1:9) How inspiring! Of course, a chapter on worry and trusting God wouldn't be complete without perhaps one of the most comforting verses of all: "And we know that God causes everything to work together for the good of those who love God and are called according to his purpose for them." (Romans 8:28)

When I become overwhelmed with worry, Romans 8:28 is what enables me to quickly return to God's reality. No matter what happens, God's got your back! If you love your LORD, Jesus Christ, fall into His arms. HE is God. HE created you and everything good in this world. HE has a plan and a purpose for you and your life. We can't see the future, but God can. We can be assured that each experience we live has a purposeful outcome. Look for the hidden meaning in each scary situation. If you can't see it now, one day you will. Trust that.

Paul writes, "Don't worry about anything; instead, pray about everything. Tell God what you need, and thank him for all he has done. Then you will experience God's peace, which exceeds anything we can understand. His peace will guard your hearts and minds as you live in Christ Jesus." (Philippians 4:6-7)

Some great advice on worry comes from Rick Warren in *The Purpose Driven Life: What on Earth Am I Here For?*[3] He explains that worry is when we think about a problem repeatedly in our minds. But if you switch your attention from the problem to Bible verses, it then becomes meditation. So if you know how to worry, you know how to meditate! Next time fear and worry are about to take hold, grab your Bible

---

[3] Warren, Rick. *The Purpose Driven Life: What on Earth Am I Here For?* Zondervan, 2002.

and read it. Find a song that allows your mind to focus on God and His love. Fixate on the good, the truth, and the life. This is the attitude antidote.

Fear is a liar.

LORD,

Let Your love cast out all my fear! I pray that Your presence will envelop all my worry. When I lose perspective and begin to travel down the rabbit hole of darkness, quickly pull me back and remind me that You are in control. Jesus, You are the Light of the world. Please flicker a light when I'm in the darkness of my own worry and fear. You alone can conquer all my fear and worry.

I have no reason to worry or fear. I am instructed to cast all my anxiety on You, for You care for me. Such an incredible God You are that You would care so much for me when my heart is full of sin. Jesus, I accept You and Your grace today. Make me clean, and restore my soul. Thank you for Your incredible sacrifice; help me not to take it for granted.

Jesus, grant me Your peace, and do not let my heart be troubled. You alone are the Creator of this world, and You are my God. My soul is overwhelmed with Your promises. You said You will be with me always, that You are my comfort. You have redeemed me, and I am Yours. Nothing will be able to take me from You. You are my light and salvation, the stronghold of my life. Whom shall I fear? No one, for I know who goes before me; it's You, LORD, the strength of my life.

Help me to not invite the devil into my heart or my home. What he brings is not what I want in my life. Worry and fear are evil gifts from him, and I will lean on my God instead.

Jesus, let those people in my life who are struggling with worry and fear know You. I pray that they would come to find You and keep You in their hearts. Your love is all I feel, Jesus. Surround me with Your love today, tomorrow, and forevermore. Thank you that my tomorrow is past and that I have a fresh new today to make my life new.

God, thank you for listening to me. Thank you for forgiving and always loving me. Thank you for Your constant presence and for

the power of Your grace to assist me in being more of who I was made to be. I ask You to be at the center of my life as I move throughout this day. As always, let Your angels watch over my family and me, keeping us safe. Let Your kingdom come; let Your will be done.

Amen,

Your Humbled Child

KEEP seeking HIM, you will find WHAT YOU'RE looking for

Day 20:
Planned Prayer

"Keep on asking, and you will receive what you ask for. Keep on seeking, and you will find. Keep on knocking, and the door will be opened to you. For everyone who asks, receives. Everyone who seeks, finds. And to everyone who knocks, the door will be opened." (Matthew 7:7-8)

This is Jesus speaking here! He is giving us one of life's secrets. We have the incredible power to write our own future, partnering with His will for us. It can be filled with great blessings, plenty of experiences, and joy—all without a bad attitude! We have the ability to live the life we've only dreamed of. We just need to want it, envision it, believe it, and then ask for it as often as we can. If we keep seeking, we WILL find. After all, Jesus said so. This is the attitude antidote.

For immediate change, we must begin to apply this practice to our lives, quickly! What's on the list? Pray about attitude. Pray it will be easy to control. Pray to always possess a joy-filled, happy demeanor. Pray as often as we think of it. Keep knocking. God will open the door to our request! While prayers about improving our attitudes are utterly necessary, the bottom line is that for lasting significant change, we need to practice fervent prayer regarding every aspect of our lives and the world.

But persistent praying takes a significant amount of time and energy! As the mother of two children under five years of age, I know all too well how difficult it is to dedicate even more time away from myself. Oftentimes, my prayer life is shoved aside, as life becomes overwhelming and my mind and body tire. Unfortunately, like me, so many people tend to fall short of regular, comprehensive prayer. Let us not be discouraged, though, for God has no prayer standards that He holds us to. He offers a model in the Lord's Prayer (Matthew 6), but there are no "rules" in talking with Him. Thank Jesus our salvation is not dependent upon how well we are able to communicate with our LORD! But we must be certain that improving our prayer lives, by dedicating more personal time to speaking with and to God, will significantly strengthen our relationship with Him, spilling over into all parts of life.

Thankfully, having lengthy prayer sessions are not the only effective way to communicate with God. In fact, long prayer times definitely shouldn't be the only time we're coming to Him! The commitment we've made to improve our attitudes is on a grand scale. Let's face it: One prayer per day isn't going to cut it! We must be in constant contact with Jesus if we are seeking any sort of lasting change. A tip I've found to be helpful is to keep a constant, open-ended talk with Him throughout the day. Ask for self-control, patience, and wisdom, and don't forget to thank Him, too. For we have been wisely advised, "Search for the LORD and for his strength; continually seek him" (Psalm 105:4).

While short texts sent to Jesus throughout the day are wonderful, to begin improving yourself and your prayer life, some dedicated time is also needed. Taking the time to organize your thoughts and to create a prayer plan will help you to be more effective in the time you take during lengthier prayers. I've found it helpful to create a prayer list to use when you want to make a date with God. It will simplify your life and will let you cover more ground with the time you spend in prayer. Here's a shortened example of my weekly prayers. You can use this list as a starting point to create your own.

Monday: Daughter #1—Her health, safety, and happiness; her friends; her future relationships; and her spiritual life
Tuesday: My mother—Her health, safety, struggles, future,

happiness, and decisions
Wednesday: Daughter #2—Same as Daughter #1
Thursday: Friends, experiences, and society/our world; all relationships; the future; strangers and enemies
Friday: Extended family—Their health, our relationships, quarrels occurring, and their future
Saturday: Myself—My attitude, health, personal growth, relationships, spiritual life, patience, and struggles
Sunday: My husband—His work, health and well-being; our relationship; his relationships and his spiritual life

From here, break each subject matter or person down into smaller parts to make them more manageable. It will not only help your prayers, but it will also help you to understand what you need when you feel overwhelmed and a negative attitude is on the horizon.

If you are left to pray each day without a plan, it often will feel jumbled and sporadic. Using a prayer plan will guide you to go deeper and wider with prayer. In addition to the weekly assigned prayer, remember to still pray for yourself, your attitude, and anything else weighing on your heart. And don't fret if there are days you feel as if your prayers aren't worth much or you didn't choose to take the time to pray. Take to heart the following:

"And the Holy Spirit helps us in our weakness. For example, we don't know what God wants us to pray for. But the Holy Spirit prays for us with groanings that cannot be expressed in words. And the Father who knows all hearts knows what the Spirit is saying, for the Spirit pleads for us believers in harmony with God's own will. And we know that God causes everything to work together for the good of those who love God and are called according to his purpose for them." (Romans 8:26-28)

Keep seeking HIM; you will find what you're looking for.

Jesus,

You have instructed me to pray with persistence. Heavenly Father, I know You have great gifts in store for me if I only ask You for them. So God, I'm asking You now! Take my life and transform it. Transform my entire being, as I struggle to keep composure when I am tested by the trials of life.

Let Your great wisdom flood over me. I need it in order to become a better spouse, a better parent, a better friend, and a better member of society. Jesus, Your life serves as my example to be a better person, and I want to be what You've created me to be. Help me in reaching my full potential as I strive to make You proud, Father. I want to be Your shining light so everyone will know through my attitude, words, and actions that You are at work in my life.

Creator, I wish to know You on a deeper level and strengthen my bond with You. Impart in me inspiration to keep my prayer life catapulting forward; I want my prayer life and my relationship with You to explode. God, when things of this life get in the way, motivate me. When I may choose to do something else, convict me. When forces actively attempt to get in my way, knock them down. When I may forget, prompt me. I will dedicate time each day to You, my Heavenly Father.

Spirit, You help me in my weakness. You are there to help me communicate with the Father. You are my advocate, and You seamlessly merge what I ask for with the Father's will. What a blessing! I invite You to take over my prayers each and every time I pray. You know my heart and what is ultimately best for my life, so I choose Your way, not mine.

God, You fortify my spirit when I read that You cause everything to work together for the good of those who love You and are called according to Your purpose. All I can say is thank you and that I've decided that Your will is my wish.

God, thank you for listening to me. Thank you for forgiving and always loving me. Thank you for Your constant presence and for the power of Your grace to assist me in being more of who I was made to be. I ask You to be at the center of my life as I move throughout this day. As always, let Your angels watch over my family and me, keeping us safe. Let Your kingdom come; let Your will be done.

Amen,

Your Humbled Child

GUARD your heart ABOVE all ELSE FOR IT DETERMINES THE the course of your life

PROVERBS 4:23

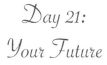

$\mathcal{W}$elcome to Day 21! Congratulations for making and completing this commitment to improve yourself and your attitude through implementing Christ-like behavior into your life. If you have taken all the principles in this book to heart and have applied them to your life, I'm sure you've seen remarkable improvements in your attitude, self-control, outlook on life, and relationships. But my biggest hope and prayer is that you have become closer to the One who created you. That your character is, was, and will continue to be refined and that you will lean on Christ in future times of trouble.

Today will be a bit different from the last 20 days. I feel compelled to help prepare you for the second part of your journey: the start of your new life with a new attitude! Before we part, I want to share something with you. While writing this book, I faced many competing forces. Visible challenges arose that ranged from mundane nuisances to blatantly outward opposition. Even at the time, it was obvious something was at work to dissuade me from composing this devotional. The only reason you're reading this now is because of the Holy Spirit's overwhelming presence. My purpose in sharing this is to reaffirm: It is not by our own will or talents that we can accomplish good things; it is only with the help of God.

Since we're concluding our journey together, I want to warn you to keep your eyes open. I'm certain that you, too, have experienced oppositional forces to improving yourself throughout this journey. Instead of being discouraged or unnerved by this, let it give you much motivational joy because who you've worked to become is a threat to the evil in this world! I urge you to keep a journal, reminding yourself of the beautiful trials you've faced and the virtuous traits you've developed. Let your new Christ-like character radiate through you every day. This is the attitude antidote.

Once the daily focus on improving your attitude ceases, the importance of what you've been working on may slowly fade away. Don't let your progress and what you've accomplished slip through your fingers! Hold on to it like it's a precious gift—because it is! What you've gained in the last 21 days is more precious than anything here on earth. You have been working on developing your spiritual maturity and your character. Be proud that you've made these changes, for fighting a negative or sour attitude takes daily commitment! I encourage you to continue to read God's Word and meet with Him daily in fervent prayer in hopes of further developing your Christ-like character.

It is no secret life is full of problems, great and small. Whenever you overcome one, another challenge inevitably will transpire. Remember: Problems allow for continual character refinement. Look to find joy and purpose in growing into a restored, more mature person who radiates Christ's light and love. So in times of trouble, remember to ultimately lean on our Holy Father, His Son, and His Spirit.

I want to end our journey together by imparting some powerful Proverbs. Keep these close to your heart, as they will provide insight, strength, and motivation in the days ahead. The book of Proverbs is a collection of biblical wisdom: "Their purpose is to teach people wisdom and discipline, to help them understand the insights of the wise. Their purpose is to teach people to live disciplined and successful lives, to help them do what is right, just, and fair." (Proverbs 1:2-3)

A favorite well-known Proverb comes from the third chapter: "Trust in the LORD with all your heart; do not depend on your own understanding. Seek his will in all you do, and he will show you which path to take." (Proverbs 3:5-6) When you feel troubled, stuck, frustrated, lonely, hurt, lost, or fill-in-the-blank—seek God first. What hope this verse gives! The LORD our God, Creator of heaven and the earth, says He will literally lead our lives if we trust in Him. We have no reason to fear, for our understanding of this life is faulty anyway. The only way to gain real understanding and peace is to place our trust in Him.

"Guard your heart above all else, for it determines the course of your life." (Proverbs 4:23) When you feel yourself going down your old path of resentment, anger, and irritation, beware and quickly turn around! Don't give in and allow these feelings to swallow you up, for you know that all they bring is hurt, a heavy heart, and a bad attitude. When your heart is filled with ugliness, you feel ill both physically and mentally. Safeguard your heart from a negative attitude with the armor of God (Ephesians 6:7-19) so you won't suffer from a sick heart, longing for hope. "Hope deferred makes the heart sick, but a dream fulfilled is a tree of life." (Proverbs 13:12)

"Some people make cutting remarks, but the words of the wise bring healing." (Proverbs 12:18) We have learned how words and a bad attitude impact others in so many ways. "A truly wise person uses few words; a person with understanding is even-tempered." (Proverbs 17:27) You can decide to be the one to bring healing instead of hurt. You have the power to make that decision! Always remember, the Holy Spirit will help you do seemingly impossible things (John 14:26). "Those who control their tongue will have a long life; opening your mouth can ruin everything." (Proverbs 13:3)

Jesus,

You've been longing for me to come back to You since the day I was born. Here I am LORD, at Your feet, humbly looking up at Your greatness. Your love is overwhelming, and Your grace is never-ending. There is no greater honor than to serve You and Your plan.

I am able to make my life here on earth better because of You. Only You can give me such strength, hope, peace, purpose, belonging, and abundant love. I ask You to come into my life and fill me with Your presence today and each day that I live. For one day I will see You again, Creator, and I want to give testament to a life that was pleasing to You. I know I can't do that on my own but only through Your grace and mercy.

Beautiful Savior, thank you for this journey. Thank you for Your Spirit who is with me at all times. You've said a person with understanding is even-tempered, so this is who I strive to become. LORD, there will be days when I don't control my tongue and fail You, but I pray for strength to overcome the temptation.

Most importantly of all: Shelter my heart and wrap it in Your power, for I stand no chance without it. With Your armor, safeguard my heart from a negative attitude so evil may not tear me apart. Keep me grounded and strong with Your truth, faith, righteousness, peace, salvation, and Your Spirit. You are the ultimate answer to winning this battle against my own self.

Once and for all, I ask You to banish bitterness from my life and to transform my attitude into a strength of mine. I trust You, and I seek You today. I will forever lean on Your understanding, for my wisdom pales in comparison to Yours.

God, thank you for listening to me. Thank you for forgiving and always loving me. Thank you for Your constant presence and for the power of Your grace to assist me in being more of who I was made to be. I ask You to be at the center of my life as I move throughout

120

this day. As always, let Your angels watch over my family and me, keeping us safe. Let Your kingdom come; let Your will be done.

Amen,

Your Humbled Child

75349098R00074

Made in the USA
Columbia, SC
17 September 2019